Esprit de Corps
Quebec Poetry of the Late
Twentieth Century in Translation

ESPRIT DE CORPS

Québec Poetry of the Late
Twentieth Century in Translation

EDITED BY

LOUISE BLOUIN   BERNARD POZIER   D.G. JONES

Cover artwork by Lucie Ranger
Cover design by Terry Gallagher/Doowah Desigh

We acknowledge the support of the Canada Council for the Arts for our publishing program.

Printed and bound in Canada

"Time Falls", "Hibernations" and "ICBM" from *The Fifth Season* (Exile Editions) by Paul-Marie Lapointe. Translation ©D.G. Jones. Reprinted by permission.
"The Hangman's Hand" from *Rose and Thorn* (Exile Editions) by Roland Giguère. Translation ©Donald Winkler. Reprinted by permission.
"Because" and "Your Phone Number" from *Evenings at Loose Ends* (Signal Editions/Véhicule Press. Translation ©Judith Cowan. Reprinted by permission.
Two untitled selections from *Categorics* (Coach House Press) by Normand de Bellefeuille. Translation ©D.G. Jones. Reprinted by permission.
"Homeland", "Apparition", "Scorched Earth", "Tenebrous Lesson" and "Absurd Sun" from *Oeuvre poétique: 1950-1990* (Éditions du Boréal)by Anne Hébert. Translation ©Daniel Sloate. Reprinted by permission of General Publishing Ltd.
Selection from *The Edges of Light* (Guernica Editions) by Hélène Dorion. Translation ©Andrea Moorhead/Guernica Editions. Reprinted by permission.
"John Coltrane", "Words That Everyone Says" and "After" from *This Desert Now* (Guernica Editions) by Yves Préfontaine. Translation ©Judith Cowan/Guernica Editions. Reprinted by permission.
Three selections from *Quartz and Mica* (Guernica Editions) by Yolande Villemaire. Translation ©Judith Cowan/Guernica Editions. Reprinted by permission.
All other selections (in their original French) ©Écrits des Forges

Editorial Offices
The Muses' Company/J. Gordon Shillingford Publishing
P.O. Box 86, 905 Corydon Avenue, Winnipeg, MB, R3M 3S3
Écrits des Forges
1497, rue Laviolette, C.P. 335, Trois-Rivières, QC, G9A 5G4

Cataloguing in Publication Data

Esprit de corps: Quebec poetry of the late twentieth century in translation

ISBN 1-896239-18-8

1. Canadian poetry (French)—Quebec (Province)—Translations into English
2. Canadian poetry (French)—20th century—Translations into English.
I. Blouin, Louise, 1949- II. Pozier, Bernard, 1955- III. Jones, D.G. (Douglas Gordon), 1929-

PS8295.5.Q8E86 1997 C841'.5408'09714 C97-900603-1
PR9198.2Q42E86 1997

TABLE OF CONTENTS

Introduction

What's been happening in French Quebec, more particularly in poetry, over the past few decades? This collection of poems by over forty poets is intended to offer the English-speaking reader at least a partial answer to that question.

Immediately one may point out that the selection of the poems was made by Louise Blouin and Bernard Pozier as part of a more comprehensive anthology of Quebec poetry from its beginnings, which has been published by Ecrits des Forges in Trois-Rivières. That is, the view of the poetry presented here is not that of the present editor but of Quebeckers themselves—more exactly, of the writers and editors associated with Ecrits des Forges.

In itself, that publication may signal a change taking place in the province. Quebec culture is no longer centered in Quebec City, as in the mid-Nineteenth Century, or in Montreal, as in the mid-Twentieth. Three Rivers, once devoted to pulpwood and lumber, now boasts a major university, attracts writers, artists and musicians, and hosts a regular international poetry festival. Ecrits des Forges and La Fondation Les Forges publish many poets, award prizes, and now present their view of the canon of Quebec poetry. Montreal still exists, with its older publishers, such as l'Hexagone, or the more recent Le Noroît and the more experimental Herbes rouges, but the view from Montreal is not exclusive or final. The poetry, perhaps the culture, is becoming decentralized.

Clearly, this collection of poems is not that of the Bloc, of some single national voice. And the reader should be warned: the title, *Esprit de Corps* , must be read with a measure of irony. The heroic narrative and epic tone of such Nineteenth Century poets as Octave Crémazie or Louis Fréchette are absent here. Even the expansive celebration of the land as a metonymical expression of a national vitality and solidarity, actual or imminent, as in Gatien Lapointe's "Ode au Saint-Laurent" or Gaston Miron's "La Marche à l'amour," is not much in evidence. We may recall the nationalism of the sixties when Miron, in a foreign country, feels the memory of his own land rise like a lump in his throat, but we may find his remark that his life is a black hole more unexpected, more striking.

When Renaud Longchamps dismisses the whole material universe as a black hole, to be abandoned for some spiritual reality, we may hear an echo of the traditional religious culture, and of Saint-Denys Garneau's dismissal of the secular world and his desperate identification with some improbable star, some absolute "beyond." But for the most part we do not find in these poems either the assurance of or the hankering for some divine or "ideal" world. Like Emile Nelligan's "Idéal blanc," the communion of saints, of the dead, evoked by Crémazie in the Nineteenth Century and, more gorgeously and poignantly by Alain Grandbois in the Twentieth, is gone—at least in its traditional Catholic or Christian or even Platonic sense. And with it has gone much of the influence of Symbolist poets, the pursuit of *la poésie pure*, even the more Surrealist concern with *le réel absolu*.

One of the few texts that voice an esprit de corps in its traditional sense is Clément Marchand's "Witnesses to the World," which dates from the last year of the Second World War. It was particularly inspired by Marchand's meeting a general of the Free French Army on a lecture tour in North America. After speaking, the General joined Marchand and others for a very good dinner; despite his extreme fatigue, he enjoyed himself so much he stayed late, stayed over, and missed what was to be his last talk in Quebec City. Within a week, Marchand learned that the General was dead, his plane shot down over Europe. According to one of our translators, Judith Cowan, the poem was an occasion for Marchand to express his solidarity with the intellectual exiles of that period, an international solidarity or awareness that he felt was often lacking in Quebec.

By the seventies, however, journalists and artists, musicians and poets were opening Quebec to the American counter-culture, flower-power and pot, as well as to the near revolution of the young in Paris in '68—along with French structuralism and post structuralism. Poetry encountered the Beats and the new Formalists, Concrete and Rock—Jazz and folksong, John Cage and Boulez, Philip Glass and Nashville. A concord of dissonance.

And the feminist movement: women's writing, from Simone de Beauvoir and Virginia Woolf to Germaine Greer and Hélène Cixous. There was actual dialogue between women writers, French and English, across Canada.

Still, if the women's movement did in fact produce a positive *esprit de corps*, it is not especially evident in this selection.

In fact, many of the poems in this selection might prompt one to translate the phrase literally, as bodily spirit—or to change it to esprit *du* corps, the spirit or consciousness of the body. "The body, we have one," says Normand de Bellefeuille in a section of his *Categorics* that is not included here: "The body, we have one that resonates with love..." Also with desire, loneliness, suffering, the anxiety and pain of death. The latter is a theme that links the present selection from Piché to Godin to Uguay. And that anxiety is generally confronted without the consolation of some conventional large faith or collective identity. The voice we hear in much of the poetry is not in the least exotic, is that of the "free" individual in a secular and increasingly fragmented society, its extreme conditions imaged in Daoust's "New York," a visual as well as aural cacophony, a material phantasmagoria, confounding body and mind, which the speaker labels simply "schizo-clinic."

To imagine is literary, says Nicole Brossard, in Quebec. To suffer is literary, to live, as a woman... Of course, we say, with our present sense of the intimate relation between discourse and "reality," this is the case for anyone anywhere. What I like is Brossard's laconic conclusion, in haste, "I am physically accustomed to existence."

While one might argue that this anthology continues what John Glassco in his anthology, *The Poetry of French Canada in Translation* (1970), called a poetry of exile, it strikes me that there is yet a more positive kind of *esprit de corps* that emerges here. It is solidarity with ordinary living, and mortal, creatures. It is early evident in Lapointe's sardonic "Time Falls," with its evocation of minorities, lost tribes, even dinosaurs—the dead unearthed by anthropologists and archaeologists. It is evident late in the book in Marie Uguay's celebration of Cézanne's oranges, and the "matter" one may finally touch or join in death. It is evident in the quiet, programmatically banal epiphanies of Charron's "mysticism of the quotidian." It is evident in Langevin's familial address to thunder and lightning, rain, wind and snow—his affectionate words for the fresh-water salmon, Ouaouaniche. It has something to do with Beausoleil's devious boast that he has, in fact, seen real pink flamingoes, and his suggestion that letters always come back to "these small objects of desire."

Let's face it: this is poetry in translation, and the reader has no doubt heard that the phrase is an oxymoron, the thing an impossibility. Alberto Manguel, at least, tells me something I haven't heard before: that in the Middle Ages "translation" was associated with transporting a saint, the relics or remains, from one place to another, sometimes illegally. He does not say if it affected the saint's capacity to bring solace or effect miracles. The translators here are not dealing with saints, but they have tried to transport a body of texts from one language to another without excessively diminishing their peculiar efficacy.

D.G. Jones
October, 1996

Rina Lasnier

The Wild Goose

When thick fogs blanket the autumn days
and the sun's eye drags bloodshot through shore drift
when polar snows cast their drowned pallor across the land
The courage-bird, born in the teeth of tundra winds
after hot matings, wing-beating in cold ocean surfs,
the goose already paired and gravid with maternal flesh
Like a new vessel taking her fill of sky and sea
glides, beside the male, wild swan in a broad double wake.

Winging milk-starred in your yearning stretch to the long
                                        flight
Winging in phalanxes lofted on intangible whitenesses
Skeins of blossom sounding the altitudes of the lesser americas
by goslings and your hearts' blood called back,
for the winds' webs can never tangle your swimming feet.

Birds family-tied and faithful to the Labrador steppe,
how long shall we hide our brooding loves in silence
like the forests' shoulders bent with snow?
How long shall cold fires mute our tongues?
Courage-birds, by the palmate prints of your paired feet
wake in us the challenge of a land precipitate of poles
and save us our wild vastnesses for birthing
and this throaty call for words in place of exile.

13

Little Eskimo Suite

I

Northern Snow

We offer no prayers to the heaviest snow
so deeply piled in forests of bristly ghosts
(snow less wounded than the tree, harder than its limbs)
from which we mould our vaulted igloos' bones,
ships unattackable in the ramparts of the wind;
may it last through the time of weddings.

We do not pray the pure and incandescent ice
or its waterline clear and straight as the knife,
or invoke the nameless maidenhead of death;
we split it with a long arterial laugh
to hear it break beneath its covering sheets.

14

II

The Eskimo Child

The baby laced in his foliage of furs
props the rise and fall of his mother's shoulders
—warmth of the sap encased in the bark—
while his eyes behold more deserts than a star.

He's learning a trail as twisted as the river
animal rage as straight as light
the lean frugality of fish chewed living
and the solitary deaths of birds and the agèd.

Leave the soft fluff of his innocence untouched
—hands bound in the swap of skinned furs—
his eyes impose the snow's will,
a robust royalty of elemental games.

III

Fire Watchers

Long snow, and spread of passive time
as night's igloo, spoked to the travelling flares
of the polar Bear, encircles the northern world:
night racked on the wheel of its star.

Under the sweating slats of ice
the eyes that watch the crumbling fire,
the skeleton dancing its red-hot jig,
see carnal summer there and the dog days of love.

Gleam of woman more devotional than oils
and her face boned with wordlessness;
mutism of fire till the laughter of fusion,
this country's forge more spellbound than the sun.

Translated by Judith Cowan   15

Clément Marchand

Witnesses to the World

Faces one is happy to greet
In the intimate glow
Of the lamps, turned low
When at evening we meet;

They join our debate,
Dear friends whom harsh fate
And high cause have whirled
From the four corners of the world;

Exiles from every country
Often with no other baggage
Than the fleeting image
Of joy, some former felicity,

And who must soon depart
Leaving a message denies
They shall ever be faint of heart,
Minds set, freed of all ties;

Faces trials don't astonish,
What will become of you
In the world's deadly skirmish,
O early pleasures your spirits knew
And dawn may well ravish?

16

I

I seal a friendship
With a shake of the hand;
Days may run like the sand,
I won't lose my grip.

No matter how long
The exchange, if the accord
Is of men of their word
It remains strong.

II

Evenings when you have claimed
My thoughts, I'm led to enquire
Toward what end the locked fire
Of your hope is, arrow-like, aimed

On what bold thought
Will your spirits have closed
Or in what renewed combat
Will your strength be disposed?

17

III

Curious, your spirits' habit,
Capricious enough, of arriving
Here in the room, palpably intimate,
To float there, half smiling.

It's but one more snare
Fate sets you. I've found
I don't instinctively turn round
To see if you're there.

I must be doubly alert
If your memory revives.
I try to keep it covert
By averting my eyes.

I feared even a glance
Might lead you to balk
On the shaky tightrope you walk
And so end your advance.

18

IV

He has remained my guest,
The man with uncertain itinerary,
Without home or land, but a patrimony
And a high quest.

Distinguished traveller,
May he persist in his planetary
Round. In my own sedentary
Heart, I keep him safe harbour.

Translated by D.G. Jones

ANNE HÉBERT

Homeland

Land received in the deepest hollow of sleep
The bitter tree grows over us
Casting its high shadow upon the awakening
Its silence on the core of words
Its name to be carved on a field of snow
And you, brought back from daybreak,
Drop this old dream along the shores of the old world
Think of our love, the honour is enough
The raw years, the candid face the eyes opened wide
Fresh water is in season no more
Woman is brackish as algae
My soul tastes of the sea and unripe oranges
Forests on the alert rivers unbound
          sing of the mother-waters of this time
A whole continent swept by storms
Let us depart, my love, the world melting like a
          city of cloth
Let the heart's fierce resemblance to its homeland
Be fulfilled.

Apparition

The giant has reached her full height
She is moving in the shadows
And her heavy step shakes the bedroom walls

She grows and stretches and spreads
Against the beams and doors
And along the ebony ceiling

Her hollow eyes gleam
Like a sunken well
Deep in the dark

Her deep breathing like an equinoctial gale
Heaves out her ivory ribs
To show her red-hot heart
Through the pallid bars
Charnel house and splendour

She doesn't slit the air or damage the night
In the thickness of the dark
She muses and stubbornly seeks

20

The thinnest of points
Wherein she'll drive her knife
The pupil of my eye

Scorched Earth

The excessive suns of these scorched lands
With their secret fervour of dead stones,

Their eyes like candles long since snuffed out
Gleam dully in the deepest hollow of the earth
Like slumbering volcanoes.

From a place of exile cold as the moon
In the ashes and the grey lava
They give off strange and secret rays

Insane birds, heads under wings,
Busily eating their hearts
That glitter
Like snow.

Tenebrous Lesson

Fall asleep on my feet
Like a tree
In the night

No eyelids no lashes
Eyes wide open
Fill with night
To the brim

The black heart of the night
Trickles upon my heart
Turns my blood
To blackest of ink

The fluid night flows in my veins
I put down roots in the black woods
Ankles shackled
Soul dissolved in the night

Absurd Sun

Yellow sun in her fist
She's called Liberty
And from where they placed her
On the highest mountain
She watches the city
As the grey pigeons keep soiling her
Day after day

Changed into stone
The folds of her cloak are motionless
And her eyes are blind
around her splendid brow a crown of thorns
      and droppings

She reigns over a people of bitter sunflowers
Blown by the wind from empty lots
While in the distance the smoking city
Turns over on its bed
And adjusts the shackles of the slaves.

23

Translated by Daniel Sloate

ALPHONSE PICHÉ

Angina

Here she is
attentive
and never far from my side
her hollow sockets following me
when I walk
her step in step with mine
Sometimes she speeds up a little
and her sinewy arms clutch me round the abdomen
tightening
till I walk on
She steps through the doorway
close beside me
and at night leans against the wall
watching me
until she comes nearer
puts her palms on the bed frame
and watches patiently
sizing me up

then she slips in under the sheets
close by my side
and lays her cold cheek
on my heart
listening to my pain
her long fingers on my carotid arteries
the last pressure
when

24

Getting Up

Delicate early first light
in sloppy slippers
venturing hopefully out into day
a season of birds
of chattering radios
and pages of the newspaper
Stubbly beard
First whisky
down a roughened throat
Night of grace
not the last
Brilliant day shakes off its cobweb shadows
and trembles
at the rediscovery of light
Soon the follies of the sun
in the flimsy skirts of women
will touch a space
of thigh or breast
ultimate sustenance
seized from the street's display

25

Dusk

Frail impulse down life's sloping surface
Images that outline a suppression of dreams
A black echo
from the well's familiar stone lip
bleeds through my heart and dies in endlessness
Now is the time of twilight down the spine's bony ridge
Towards some Horn and faery shipwreck
far from shore
The tall ships have vanished into the purples
of night

Huge echoing sheds
still ringing with the trample of peoples
gape to the winds off the water
captive space with winches coiled
walls wood and brass
and halted wanderings
all raise their signposts over the flooding of the past

Old age's solstice
backyard of decrepitude
a gasping garden plot
of pretty sprouts and suffering roses

Chalky and impassive the face
of sharp-edged gilt religiosity
over the heart-skipping hours of fear

The End

The last station, wicket closed, no heat
End of the line
Its stumps of wheelstops rusting in the lichens
The times come round to the hospice doorway
Names called from the file
And walls closing in
Dawn of the last night
Yellow-skinned wrinkles round the rictus of dentures
The secret stink of defecations
The syringe and the dry agony
Death's dirty fingers clutching at the fringe of life
Class distinctions of the coffin
Angle of the head panel
For an ochre face in a muslin frill
The people
The cloths and metal vessels of the liturgy
The black procession to the graveyard
The iron lintel the open gates
And jagged line of tombstones on the sky
The shovel in the earth
The grave's wound folded on eternity
The people

Translated by Judith Cowan

Gilles Hénault

Song of the Cigarette Ashes

I

She went and left behind her ashes.
And why not? Fire has no history
And continents are enriched by the fine art
        of smoking.
What say you, elves of the magic day?
Those times are over since the soul proclaims
            in you
The blossoming of pernicious voyages.

II

She went and left behind her ashes.
Transparent is the flight of smooth ships
sailing along a memoried horizon
where the ceaseless oar wipes out the waves of dream.
She went without her golden fish and their cherry hearts
without the light from rainless days
without the noisy cloak the trains weave as they pass
without the little red riding-hood of vanishing suns
without the bear cub seated amidst the desolation of the
flood.

III

She left walking backwards
her youth undone
leaving behind the fish like a fruit.
The knife is not so sharp as bursts of laughter
The convulsed face is a very bright screen
The first day she made a spring
        flow from her hair
You remember
The second day was a day of cloudless love
        on the islands of summer
And the other days were caravan-days
The orients would pale before the two-headed monster
And the last day she left
with her ashes behind her
and her bag of misinterpreted pranks
Her hair in the keyholes
Her fingerprints on the ceiling
Her broken bursts of anger
at the place where the wind of years to come
blows in.

Translated by Daniel Sloate

GASTON MIRON

Our Slumbers

Such are the heavens in carnal fields
with you they light up the earth our
unconscious
                    —film behind dreams—
fills and releases of the non verbal
your left leg between mine your sex
hot on my thigh locked till dawn's
desire   ivy run wild   warmth inspired

so distanced despite me we repose
airborne as in Chagall and of all time

TGV Lyon

Among so many wasted steps in Lyon
my own rushing me off to the level
of this train station bench where she sits
myself swept away in the bustle then on the platform
her smile flickers within my wild gaze
end of the credits flashing by blurred

You are far from home   Archaic Miron
where it's like here the cold of the world
within and Quebec always that
rises in your throat

gripping the heart

Respite

That's what I think: the world lacks reality
I'm made up of the black holes of the universe
on occasion   sometimes   in some part
of the landscape there stirs a splendour before your eyes
resting there in its migration
and diminishing the bitterness of being human

Padua

Things are far away, people and the world
always somewhere far ahead
in the dark regions of age
but one day walking close to me among the others
you just up and slid your hand under my arm
this gesture long time so foreign to me
there, once again too late, eternity had come back to me
and almost in the same moment despair
will you ever forget Rossana Carrer the light in your eyes

when our side-glances locked
the time it takes to cross the street in the rain in Padua
long time I loved you at Treviso
before ever seeing you
and, from this very day on, never
shall I see you again

Translated by D.G. Jones

33

Gilles Vigneault

Nocturne

On the white naked page
The words refuse to come
But what's this small black dot
Where did it come from

And now it rises up
And climbs into the air
Is that you Madame spider
What are you doing there?

In vain you spend your night
In spinning out your thought
Such work will come to naught

To truly sing and write
Needs neither toil nor art
Consult your broken heart

for Félix Leclerc

Would that every instant's word
Were everything to everyone
But when we scan the window-screen
What is becomes what might have been

Only the silence between the letters
Steals in and in its secret way
Very slowly establishes
A little time within the space

It's always beginning over
Though it never lasts for long
It's always ancestral effort and
It's child's play too, that's a must

Language is a larger land
Than any ever promised us

35

Fountain

My pretty looking eyes
Popped out one day by chance
And shattered like faience
At the white sound of your voice

And in your tight closed hand
I found the pale blue spheres
Whose lacklustre veneer
Conceals the secret scope

Of fabulous mystic springs
That gush forth evenings
Like a big bouquet of hope
To the wonder of the sands

Song

I made my sky from a bit of cloud
And my forest from a reed.
The longest voyage I ever took
Was on a water weed.

With a little cement I made a town.
With a mud puddle, the sea.
With a stone I made my island
An icicle winters me.

And every one of your silences
Is an everlasting goodbye,
Each moment of indifference
Contains a lover's sigh.

So when I dare to offer
Your beauty this single rose
In the rose you will discover
All summer's garden holds.

37

Translated by Philip Stratford

Roland Giguère

Love Delight Calliope

Love delight calliope
barefoot in a garden of flight
yesterday wrote my way to blood
today I write calliope love delight
to target the heart
down the road that twists the most
knotted knotty
the road with the pitted stones
to fetch up where we are
not very far
a bit to the left of virtue
a bit to the right of crime
that's left an enormous rusty stain
on our fresh-washed clothes in the sun
                        on the line
and gets us where
I'd be glad to know
to the flip side of rust
delight calliope love
or just just just to the heart?

just.

The Hangman's Hand

Giant hand that weighs us down
giant hand that pins us to the ground
giant hand that snaps our wings
        hand of hot lead
        red hot iron hand

giant nails that rake our bones
giant nails that pry our oyster eyes
giant nails that stitch our lips
        scorched enamel nails
        nails of rusted tin

but comes the gangrene
gangrene
gangrene

the giant hand that binds us to the earth
will rot
the joints like crystal crack
the nails come unstuck

the giant hand will decompose
and we will rise and take ourselves elsewhere.

Translated by Donald Winkler

Paul-Marie Lapointe

Time Falls

(earth is our menace
at the corner of the street, each noon,
the same well-fed face
the assurance of the passing parade
the fanfare
and all the dead that hole in the heart…)

time falls
families showers gusts of sparrows

time falls
    a lost tribe floats up to the surface
    children of the pyramids of the sun
    amphoras of dust corn and furs
    cliffs of the dead
    (cliffs like hives from which the gorged
      souls of the death-eaters whites
        take wing)
    stupefied family

time falls
    Abenaki Maya Birmingham Negro
    civil souls of my dead savages
    anger interred in the dung heap
      of horses of prey
    in the knowledge of soldiers and saints
    in the armed frigates
    for the swooning delight of an infanta and
      the pathos of a tribute to the unkown
      soldier

time falls
    in the month of the salmon the villages
      are installed the municipal offices
    the fishermen and anglers
    the capitals polished with death's hand

time falls

 slave galleys
 Atahualpa
 today's savages
 wiped out
 (Cinderella palpitating in silk her three
  square meals her prince
 O peaceful sleep
 round earth where the houses all alike
  wink out
 one day to the next it may come the final rest)

time falls

 the small men of prehistory eddy
 between the buildings
 in the rain freighted with missiles

time falls

 satisfied species

41

Hibernations

within you I let fly white birds

few birds are white apart from doves
unless they've wintered here
planted like crosses in such space
a dryness unfolding a deployment of shivers
as strange as the snow itself
has it we ask one care except to light on us
                              on the villages
                              on the cages
between the stones the straws sculptured by the wind

our dead do not fly off
unless within ourselves
                  as do the children we have
who make their way in the interior

white birds   and airy skeletons

ICBM

each day astonished you land up on earth
this night was not the last

but the brontosaurus
and Caesar
and the Incas
and the Crow circling

soft watery world
the craters erupt
      embryonic cry

the Cloud like a toad squats on its earth
squeezes it with small repeated hugs

mother of dust

the wild goose makes it from the Andes in spite of
                        the radar

on nylon catwalks flung
between worlds
sway the delicate haunches of girls

soft watery world welter of corpses

day breaks bad but I know in getting through it
                      it is not the last

a bombadier stretches out at your side
your nights are secure!

O President O Good Shepherd
General of the Islands and the Moons

the children curl up like burnt leaves

43

Black Angel

black angel who is no one's skeleton
unless of winter in its every crystal
unless of the weasel in its icy appetites

the dark articulations of desire
attachments of the rose
under the rind of the cold they ripen a ferocious passion
wings of blood

Month of the Salmon

braid of pitchpine quelling the spasm
the totem bursts in the heart of the spawn
in the arabesques of egg and scale

O floriated fish
O mallard unfurled in the whirlwind

the idol will deal severely
with the blast furnace
rust in the soul
fragile robot perverting time

Translated by D.G. Jones

Janou Saint-Denis

We Are

one 8th of March (1977)

the blind alley,
a threat to destiny,
the breakdown of the sentence,
seducers at the gallows,
the intent of love,
the shore where penny pinchers quarrel,
burning affectations,
merit with patience,
the fantabulous star,
the dead slander,
the challenge of the juggler,
bitterness led astray,
vigilant gloom,
the lenient membrane,
sacrificial filth,
the immortal landlady,
the waifs of blunder,
a foaming crutch,
the flowering of cleansing spume,
unburdened morality,
the dispassionate wound,
the pride of the gods,
the chill of the shadows,
endless mischief,
mindful of fractures,
the chalice of blood,
the belated slap,
the loop in the spiral,
the suddenness of ether,
unruffled flu,
the laughing stock of the mundane,
a crib of docilities,
the capture by heart,
a frenzy of scrolls,
obscene gentleness,

the wicked branch,
the leader's headdress,
the beaming skein,
eggs in turmoil,
the antlers of the masses,
pregnant truces,
a feast of misfortune,
generous latitude,
the male's litter box,
the caress of expectation,
an earmarked victim,
the ambrosia of fiction

From the icon to the monument,
we are the laughter of a grass snake,
the hiccup of a mouse,
the leap to overcome and

SPACE TO RECREATE

so that
Québécoises et Québécois
ignite in one passion,
join in tenderness.

47

Like a Little Girl

Like a little girl
  she does what she is told not to do
  she drinks so that someone will say
  I'm thirsty for you—stay with me

Like a little girl
  she plays with what can harm her
  yet she knows
  she plays she plays with just anyone
  she plays so that someone will intervene
  don't play that way
  you're going to hurt yourself

Like a little girl
  she lives as she can
  somewhat by procuration
  she lives she lives
  in any old way
  she lives there or elsewhere
  it depends on
  who can live with her

Like a little girl
  she loves and she claims it
  at once
  she loves she loves
  it happens every time
  at the height of passion

Like a little girl
  feigning wisdom
  like a woman
  attentive and tender
    she sees

she plays she lives she loves
fabulous and irritating
  this little girl

somewhat herself
somewhat me
somewhat you

    serious and rebellious
    laughing at norms
she drinks from a glass too large for her

Like a little girl
    searching for her place
    in the heart of the world
      of grownups

Translated by Monique Martin

49

DENISE BOUCHER

All the Day Long

So you've been
to the country where
three blueberries
make a pie
and the other where
the mosquitoes
go strawberry picking
along side
what did you think
of the fireflies
did you hear the loon
on the shore
but above all else
you've returned
so happy with whales
you've ended up
unable to fathom what's absolute
about Moby Dick

50

*

Sugar pink
the nails
of the left hand
placed high
on the page
the colour really
goes well
I really should
stock up
the other hand writes
I never want
to be without it

this pink softens
the brown spots
one look at it
and there's no lingering
elsewhere

Life Size

Anne-Laure
you have a name
to inspire songs
with the refrain
of your eleven years
and the zest
of childhood
which leads you to cling
to your rabbits
still and the mini-skirt
of your mother
and the water-
bottle you bring
to your father
at the end of the field
Anne-Laure
in Auneau
riding your bicycle
in a way that might show
you dream California
we who tremble
before the things that remain
with the milk of your childhhood
will like them
watch you as you go

*

For you five-year-old
Samuel
already a big
land owner
we don't sow
little stones
you know the
coming and going
how to use
the droopy chestnut's
small branches you
bring to your mother

to kindle
the fire in the morning
what image
will you patch together
of us who
went along without
holding hands
yours reaching for
a kleenex
to snuff up your terrible cold
and three times
as many American
cherry
coughdrops in case
I in your fever
burn what I can't swallow
listening to your account of the world
before you were born
six languages at least
spring from your mouth
from that of your clancestors
and your father and mother
to that of the astronaut
whose photo you use
to demonstrate the height of
the William pear tree
Samuel you have the assurance
of those who are bound
to inherit, well
land and
will be able to go all the way
to the Moon

52

Translated by D.G. Jones

SUZANNE PARADIS

Web

Go ahead vertigo-free and retrace the flesh
the journeys it embarked upon
through sweat blood and a hail of dreams
in the abolished luxury of its millenia
and its lightness at the tip of the tongue

Only in the echo and the ash can you recognize
its cavalcades crowned with dust
paths cast pell-mell in all directions
like a web
soon coagulated in shards of glass

Do not tremble at the noise or the languor
of its remembrances nor at the sheathing
of waters that it broke in the loins of women
nor at the hearsay of such creation
nor at the wound in their flank that forever flares up

Clinging to the haze of a cunning eye
go ahead relentlessly in its phlegm and bird lime
and the soul that keeps on stripping and subduing it

53

Belonging

Better to build up in the mountains
you were still wondering yesterday
amidst sap and colour

In a tumble of waters
to plot the village the tribe
and the flock that will follow it

At that altitude to plan a road
and the coveted summit
between the bramble and the legend

May the height and thickness be explored
the wines the fruit the wings
offered for tasting

To be born from the magma of their silks
leaves of copper
as if their seasons were all excessive

54

Under the kissing of birds of prey
to emerge from the egg in deepest mystery
in order to open the eye of the mountain

Bite

Forever guests of this hunger for fevers
gardens full of melons honey and endives
which grow under your nails and in the white of the eye
for red snow which dries like bread
on lips which chap and taste of sea

You never finish with winter the cold
the howl of wolves the bite of otters
the enticing gallops of sagittaria
hunger leaps and confounds them and eviscerates them
under your eyes
Their skeletons freeze
at each jolt of the soul each suspended breath

Hosts you never stop following
trails scents and wild animals
in their panting and the sweatiness
of the ground that gives way
From one bivouac to another you sow
the steady pupils of the predators
the moment their sense of smell is aroused

As a Memory

Don't forget the crumbs on the wax table
don't leave around
the scraps for the dogs
who followed their master and won't come back

Neither tomorrow nor maybe

Think of the cold in the city now
where the wet desert of streets endures
as well as the soliciting of low lamps
Before you go close the windows

Because one always hopes—a touch of perfume
that lingers on lips fingers
and elicits at any time
a memory saliva
take time to erase the tracks the imprints
and the cyphers sealed in snow
Any prowler could detect them there

56

But most of all beware of the sense of smell
of those dogs you have so perfectly trained

Translated by Arlette Francière

YVES PRÉFONTAINE

John Coltrane—Ten years after his death

Beauty
of a blackness of negro sun
        exploded in the ultimate roar
                rut of death
of androgynous blackness
            flowers of sound

Yesterday and tomorrow
        I remember
        (Oh how I remember in
        my country which remembers nothing)
I remember well   how well in the night
            our bodies
        porous with music and good
        in the warmth of your breath

You saturated space
and the tissue of our lives
demiurge
        negro
            killed twice at the front rather than once
            killed in the torment of telling all
                    at the frontiers of cry

I loved you   you never knew   you never
I loved you more than poem or speech
                    dead grasses
            facing the torrent of your signs

Coltrane-my-friend-pure-negative-of-my-snow-white-

                            photo
        sufferings of ebony as in Stravinsky's
        concerto
        for petty bourgeois figuring their fractions
        of guilt on the Stock Exchange   of horror

Beauty
      slaughtered god
            black suffering *without limits*
                  like the slave-trading sea

What I loved in you
      was the very essence of song
      that breaks the executioners
Although the executioner has survived

God-negro-America   a bitter marmalade
and you   you, your too-brief wizardry stopped
      short   like that
as if you had nothing more to say   you
      Love Supreme

And I weep   Trane
I am your own blues ringing out for help "Naïma"
for help "Africa" and I refuse   and refuse again
         despite time mocking me
your death and my death   in yours

One day perhaps I'll learn to hear
      the hidden laugh
          under your blue cascades
to live on and love you better
and carry you along till the end

Words That Everyone Always Says

Words,
words, spoken every day by everyone
and I, among the spectres   I shouted them out
                            unknowingly

I shouted them out to any heavy-imaged woman.

And   a spectre to myself   I hollowed out forms,
and wrought great raucous chants,
and exhausted myself in very ancient wars,
        forgotten rituals.

Words,
Ceaselessly I shouted out words

And I crawled   familiar of thorns and
        exploded countries
          where no one lingers,
and I crawled in the shadow of a shadow filled with
                           knives
and I crawled beneath winds blacker still blacker
        than the very thickness of absence,
and I crawled to the clinging water that resembles you.

Words.
The words   *I love you*
and I do not want to die far from your hands
        for that would be dying twice.

59

After

There was
There is
There will be
maybe
—for nothing is less certain than the lifetime of things
in this moment of the world wherein I speak to you—
a blade of grass still pushing up
among the stumps and stones
where there's nothing else left at all
but that one green blade
                    with one little thought
                            in its green head.

Translated by Judith Cowan

GÉRALD GODIN

Portage

And now I come to another portage for you
my clinging tendril my knotted vine
my bundle of nerves
with a poem slung across my chest
and the birchbark burns of the canoe
on my shoulders
yet I feel no weariness
with you
and when the wind tears their whiteness
     from the apple trees
I roll you in last summer's grass
all dressed in skin
so that for a little while you leave my life
with the marks of my teeth on your neck

61

Montreal Tango

Morning, seven-thirty in the Montréal métro
and it's full of immigrants
they do get up early
these people

so maybe the city's old heart
will beat again
thanks to them

this city's tired old heart
with its spasms
its embolisms
its heart murmurs
and all its faults

with all the reasons in the world it must have
for stopping
for giving up

62

Because

Because every atom of every object
makes a point of contradicting him
coat sleeve jacket sleeve
every atom of every shirt button
every atom in every knot in every necktie
every atom of every bootlace
because all the software
of every act of daily life
has exploded in his planetarium
because he runs into
every doorframe
with his left shoulder
because the neurons directing word traffic
are giving him gridlock
and often his words come out
bumper to bumper like five o'clock commuters
when he tries to speak
because food falls from the left side of his mouth
when he chews
because he spends his days
looking for things
that are not even lost

Your Phone Number

"What, you've forgotten my telephone number?"
"Listen, old friend, I think you know
they removed a tumour from my brain
as big as a mandarin orange
and I'm afraid your phone number
was in it."

Translated by Judith Cowan

MADELEINE GAGNON

Fleeting
thoughts
an image
several
nothing's going on everything happens
sonorous echoes no sense
music from voices lost regained
chaos in working order
murmurs
coming
from oblivion

from *The Immemorial Infanta*

Leaden moon January 3, in the belly of a swarm of bees, by the side of the road, rolling in a ball, no longer seeing, no longer hearing everything around, I knew nothing of it, I still didn't know that you had to be dead, I didn't see you no longer moving, it was a banal day, the end of an early vacation, in the afternoon I had run errands, then the bank and a few minor chores so the house would look nice while I spent the winter writing, I remember a project, a vague idea for a book, a few stories related by the same childhood haunt, a readable fantasy, a novel, finally smooth, finally continuous, in my ignorance I dedicated it to you because I would have been the godmother of your first child, you remember you spoke of a male child because you would have borne a god. And then your death closed this bible of a new era and the perfect novel once again will not take place.

Translated by Andrea Moorhead

JEAN ROYER

from *Depuis l'amour*

You the first to recognize me
in the connivings of our deep conviction
I was but tenderness attentive
to childhood music
in the largesse of your gaze become mine
without love's warfare
we dwell in a new body
who are we in the orb of desire
we bathe in the same river
where recognizing what changes us
having traveled to the tip of the star
we are learning about time which feeds
on the memory of mouths
a Chagallian foresail is taming our shadows
I see you the light eqestrienne of our games
in the embrace of words that touch us
your voice covers the silence of my voice
freed from fear
shelters us like bark in the frost
what wells strange in our bones is only
the feeling of living in a great nest of springs
so our necklace of fears is unstrung
our eyes like lichens
we have come back from beyond the cold

67

it behooves me to love you
in our more outrageous moments we wager
we are the outlook of the times
whereby we live baroque and ourselves
in its compass vast
at the winds
we are not a country but its breath
its fur and we dwell in the landscape
broadcast from our souls
which tell us the bitterness of defeat
does not impugn the loves of the great river
in which the wellspring of the poem is clarified
we are the celebration of a people without memory
become strangers to winter's straightjacket
what outlook will correct the future
if not that of the courage to love
our story defies the end of history
against my father's melancholy
composed of memory and rage
I inscribe what consumes us
are we becoming anachronisms my love
anemic and of no account
in our feel for existence
are we to live simply in love itself
together each day while this people dies
if they love us without loving themselves

68

you are the enigma of my life, its gathered
beauty, an endless interrogation
woman wife of our one truth
our love wipes out the images of love
revealing little by little some primal tie
we are learning what indeed we are
two happy solitudes in the one
quiet passion for that accord
I see you writing your fate and loving me
who are you in your own life without mirror
your poetry without distracting me from my own
voice comes to me as a possible
happiness and your body
in its fleeting eternity
I am no longer alone in my blood
through you I inherit my own life's inexhaustible
tenderness intimacy's caress
in which to discover oneself at the root of the cry
then in wakefulness being together
blind and ravished one with the other
in the scorched garden of our memories
our life sings itself out to the end of song
I give you the words of my time
the country closes its hills I enter into you
it is our future that begins...

69

Translated by D.G. Jones

Paul Chamberland

You Exist Because of Me

you exist because of me
and my face is dark as death

not even the winter chickadee
knows the hand that feeds it

there where the stream runs dry
my heart beats whole, fails not

matrix of suns
I feed on dead leaves

Be Clear as Spring Water

be clear as spring water
run with the downslope
wherever it goes
death's but a passing
and pure loss sings
itself unsung

pure loss shuns the shadow's rictus:
sun-abducted, it glories, soars

Idleness

for Yves Boisvert

sometimes you inch so near the brink
that serious thought seems nothing more
than the mulling over and over of what's obvious—
someone in us wants to end it all,
knows how and why:
door open, the sun runs in
with the wind—and only a child's
impatience is whole enough
to bear comparison
with the "hold, enough" that dismisses
demands for proof like so many lies—
as though having plumbed the solemn source of itself
there's nothing for thought to do but to twiddle
      its thumbs

Translated by Donald Winkler

GILBERT LANGEVIN

The Odd Farewell

I

Serene and exempt from risk
he's as if neutered
it's the cusp of life and his voice
knows nothing more can ever come of its echo

yet within he casts about
mulls over old delights
relics of fleeting godsends
gone for good

sworn foe of arid land
from his retreat deep in his lair
does he dream he might one last time leave the ground
      and soar?

II

Thunder our father
lightning my brothers
my sister rain cousin snow
you who graze the air
with zest
who shift the wind's path
north south west east
I bring you cordial greetings
a sprig of laughter between my teeth

Ouananiche

You mount the current of our long loves
your fins infused
with lithe enticement
emblem of these waters, you herald the waves

ouananiche ouananiche
you stitch up our dreams
coax smiles from the very stones

goddess can it be
such strong complicity
can come from a simple play of lines?

ouananiche ouananiche
you are no cheerless fish
limp-gilled, bobbing for crumbs,
swimming in place

adventure is risk
and no fear lurks
behind those heart-tugging scales
when you're dying to live

the bait we cast your way
is the price you pay for your passion
for hook and fly

now all that's left alas
is to see you bite into death
and flaunt your agony
in multi-hued hue and cry

now your jaw in flame
now a mortal flash
and a stygian cloud
makes the cool afternoon its own

then the water grows calm
where the blueberries grow
and the fisherman, sinner,
serene, remains alone

74

ouananiche ouananiche
you whom they call the little stray
across the crests and bones of years
thank you for your company

Translated by Donald Winkler

Pierre Chatillon

Washing

to wash the earth
once and for all
wash it clean of all its ills
deaths, wars
and hang it out at last
on a cord of light
between sun and moon

Every Day

Every day I leap
from one star to another
pack my bags
and soar into space
seeking in vain the door
that leads out of the universe
I pitch my tent
on unknown soil
hoping for rest
saying to myself: "Good, now
I've come so far
they'll never find me"
but every night one of the soldiers
picks up my scent
storms my sleep
takes aim
and fires on my heart

Traps

I set traps on the snow
to catch words
words warm as fur:
sun-born creatures, russet and rare
warm words with long rays for hair
that have found their way to my plots of death
chilled, I stroke the skins of words
I dress myself in their coats
and savage and hard
where time's snow falls
I stand upright
wrapped in my cloak of work
a warm coat made from wordskin

Formula One

I race the Formula One
of wanting to be elsewhere
my monococque beams its way full speed
round the Milky Way's sleek track
faster! higher!
swifter than time
that's stuck in its pit stop
I'm a shooting star glazed with hard fire
daredevil with words
going for heaven's Grand Prix
in a racing car built from verse
bisecting the night
hurtling electric with bursts of light
to the finish line
faster! faster!
and the gamble pays off
I'm crowned for all time
sun's champion
resplendent with light and champagne

Translated by Donald Winkler

Michel Beaulieu

Remember

I'll bury your memory,
within the sprawled net of a retiary
I'll sever your glass bonds

you murmur in the half-light
with the voice of the wall
with the voice of the plaster
the rope knots itself in your bones

a terrified nest the lair of blood
you wallow in flesh left high and dry

has the foreboding been talked about
has it been revealed on your back
for the terror
the horizon
the uproars

there is
no
(nothing)

a touch of water under the bark a touch of nothing
the half-light you can hear it
sliding in the eyes

I sink into your renewed shadows

there is so much time
so much lots of time a long time
night passes and its abyss

gelid joy
purple uncial

the surface was marked with a gardener's line
and chasms chapped the skin

this little nothing over indefinite space

nothing moreover that you don't grasp
and let drop from the teeth of laughter
the jaws weighed down by the horizon

moreover you speak
of an unreasonable morning
you inspect the cargo
in the wind the moorings snap

you are thrown to the deep
old pals
the holds barely contain you

remember

even though the powder in your eyes blinds you
remember

outside rain ices the brick

An Afternoon Facing the Sea

Beware of this fire: walls below walls
and the walls hatch the mirrors (o little heart
in the white bereft of mast
the foam of the waves
the sand
the rising tide of the sun in one eye
—burnt flesh—irate hair
a touch of salt/ a touch of iodine/ a touch
of water this lunar month)
it can only be good to repeat it now
and again
somehow or other (for oneself or others)
you'll never repeat it enough
a bit too much but far too much
holes in the walls (poor little
crippled memories: the thread thins out so does the net:
now you'll trap nothing but shadows
arrived from afar/ right away gone again
following the weft or the network)
I waited (you waited/ he waited) no
not any more (those fireflies)
(the batting of eyelashes on dust
or against a smidgin of nothing
you keep trotting out the flavours in your nails)
tomorrow would come/ its processions/ its tomorrows
another day somewhere would fade away

Haruspices

it doesn't look like the tea towel of the heart is ablaze
unless another steals its anonymous
secret your hair I won't speak of it yet
nor say whether it's dense as wool or steel
let it suffice to reveal it tumbles down
at the very least in the imagination which errs

sometimes

it tumbles down like a horseshoe cataract
if one deciphers in a few centuries the corners
would you happen to catch yourself cursing those hands
if amidst the misty flowerings of the night
those hands did not discover you yet nor your curls
and yet you may nonetheless marvel
at discovering some quiver in your shoulders
but the vanishing point in your eyes I'll discover soon
so that the colours won't catnap in the hands
nor get tangled in branches the fragility of ropes
where the trapped bird-catcher trapping his very light

prey

did let them escape from his trembling fingers
or some other cypher no sooner traced than effaced in

space

and you will ripen in the night with a trenchant taste

Translated by Arlette Francière

FRANCE THEORET

A Bundle of Nerves

The enormous price one has to pay
for being an individual
can never adequately be decried.

Hubert Aquin

I will utter your cries. I utter your cries. You protest, crying.
Are you these cries? I will be your cries. I am your cries. You
write now that you have not cried, will you utter these cries?
There is, you say, here and now, nothing more. You endorse
the present, wide and high, a tropical sun. Reason, pain. Pathos
to master again and again at the word's core. Writing is the antithesis
of cries, even sounded it's a silent voice. Every word grafted onto
my language has been put to death. I write unto forgetfulness,
I write towards you.

84

*

To become human you must anticipate all-out assaults that stem
from outlandish rumours, an ever unpayable debt (that of being
born), throbbing pain, indwelling snares, emotional chaos and
delirium. Do violence to feelings and you will engender beings
forever bereft of lucidity. Learn that every word's source is a cry
and you will give yourself over to the first master happening
past. Or the single defensive tongue. The strong live thus. I herald
the "you" that's a bundle of nerves, those voices set like mines
long long ago. For on festive occasions of slack-jawed happiness,
all of humanity wishes itself well. We will deal harshly with fine-
honed words, to speak (in your opinion) requires community.

*

Who can soak up words, authentic tears and entreaties that worm their way in as though invested with their own intelligence? I exist outside time and place, bound to my body's weight, forever writ down in advance, shattered, split between a mighty delirium and what's spuriously rational. Let my mourning be forgetfulness. Our species' savagery is mine indeed. It is my voice, slow and hoarse. Vivisection of the tongue, balance and harmony forever lost, a nostalgia that is utterly feminine. We're in the world, I'm of the earth. Gravitation is not the only law. I am born of energies ceaselessly renewed.

Translated by Donald Winkler

85

Pierre Morency

I Do Know

That one day I'll die
that it will be cold inside my shirt
and suddenly I'll feel my feet are wet
and strange animals are crawling into my ears

I'll have missed an appointment
killed without meaning to
as oftener and oftener I do

to get away I'll travel incognito
through the belly of an underground city
it'll be evening, about nine o'clock
a deathless war will just have finished
while a terrible peace sees the light to bed
and women will come crowding round me
singing that man returns through them
three children will trundle the moon in a wheelbarrow
over the sidewalks of the underground city
where a bird will be dying
in a ventilation shaft
and it'll be cold inside my shirt

86

I Should Tell You

I should tell you right now that my arrival in this world was no ordinary
birth, by passing through a woman's body. No. It began on the day when I
found myself nestled in the belly of a plane. I was no baby, I was a bomb.

And I'm thinking back now to that day when I was a bomb. As you can
imagine, it's not easy to be a bomb. There's not much future for a bomb.

I can only just recall the day the plane flew over my house. All that comes
back is a sudden feeling of freedom high up in the air, then of spinning,
nose downward, until just above our neighbourhood, where I changed to a
great flash. I must have killed a lot of people when I fell, but I've never
known. No one has ever mentioned it. What I do know though, is that a day
came when, fragment by fragment, a bit of shrapnel from the grass, a
shard found in a woman's blood, a splinter from the river, a splinter from
the city's life, a day came when, bit by bit, I put myself back together.

And now, in the steel of my being, a kind of life is starting to rumble, so
that once again, I'll be opening up, in a fracas of light and blood.

Translated by Judith Cowan

Nicole Brossard

Contemporary

there where life inflicts pain
in fits and starts
there is no death
just the flux of light
our gift for heightening beauty

Native Land

in Quebec to imagine is literary
and to weep, wander, begin again
in Quebec, to be a woman
and weep, wander, begin again
to die is very easy, often
you find a woman who has been wounded
in the course of happiness

Echo

suffering for you is literary
because life often seems the same
as something read, that pain
life asks no leave to negotiate
books or the body
silence simplifies suffering
to speak is a different thing
for women

Customs

the lovely measures we take
to outflank death
not forgetting
the violet disquiet in our eyes
while we talk
and nod our heads in complicit code
summing up on the run
I am physically accustomed to existence

Translated by Donald Winkler

Francine Déry

Danger Café

I am no longer part of this unbearable city.
I roam through it unable to see it.
I arrive at the docks. And dream.
Ships hoisting flags from the ends of the earth
drop off their alien cargoes.
Elsewhere, there is hope in the reverberation of words.
In the rasping of pulleys alongside the docks.
Elsewhere.
I write it on the surface of the water.

A girl of sixteen, I blast my ears
with raucous music.
Tonalities of rare pearls anchored in a dog's collar,
Andalusian maybe.
When it rains on this city, it pours raw despair.
Let's move on.

Two long dusky legs.
A man's raincoat. Hands in pockets.
Satisfaction.
I am elsewhere. Twenty years old.
All pores arriving at the port are there to savour
every cube and every square of the unknown cipher.
Women gathering. Discourse.

And desire becomes pleasure.
The lover. The lover's collaboration.
Let's imagine. A simple diversion.
There will be hands like...
It will happen one night out of...
We will enjoy the odour of...on...

And our mingled cries in a ritual of our own devising.
Place your bets.
The stakes would be exorbitant. I was lost.
Elsewhere. I dream of...
Obstinately long legs. Dusky legs.

I will be Tintin reporting from the ends of the earth.
Impassioned full moon over uprisings in the kitchen.
Hey! Girls, what if we ignited the revolution.
What if we exploded the hell out of stupidity.
It happened at 1960 Street of the Cuban Republic.
It was there we shared disorder.

It's at thirty that women begin to know
the dark side of creativity.
Words activate a limitless dimension.
Disorder signals the devouring of passion.

The dream expanded within the threatening stillness
of the unturned page.
From my favourite window, I survey the consistency
of the imaginary.
It's at thirty that women begin
dreaming dangerously.
While watching sinking ships.
While unleashing the toxic blue flowers
still floating in the cup of their youth.
Elsewhere.
The years copulate with other drunken ships
that carry me away.

Forty years?
Guard the secret combination that permits
evasive entry into countries behind the dream curtain.
Elsewhere. I write it the same way as I always have.
And I take a holiday in Cuba.

Black coffee on days where I no longer dream.

Translated by Sonja Skarstedt

Célyne Fortin

To Write in Abitibi

was it snowing flowers
the wild cherries changed season
you hardly heard the birds
eyes locked on childhood

to write in Abitibi
—others go to Paris—
to rediscover childhood
its smells its sounds its lights
the precise remembered place
the hearth you entered with life
the journey
from the village here to the city
from childhood here to womanhood
a whole story to be recovered

to write in La Sarre
to write a woman's story
to read the story of Quebec women
wanting to be part of History
to admire the boldness of these women
their strength
to share their hopes
inscribing energy fervour
what have I come here to look for
a link perhaps
one that binds me to my mothers

this *I* wants to know
who she is
this *I* still doesn't know very well
where she is going
this *I* that every evening is a bit
less lively
this *I* that every day is a bit
more loving

a long time afterward
still to remember
the kitchenware and its music
hands and their tiredness
on the stairs on the shutters
the men's shirts

memory made domestic
you will return
to this aspect of things

*

to see Abitibi again
spread out under snow
to push ahead ever further
in the greys of this land
to rediscover the ghosts
of the time when one was young
to dig up the memory
of unknown time

hard to fill this page
where the writing won't flow
there is the heaviness
of the hand on each word

is it really him
my father
in this dated photo
and the lumber camp's epic
and my mother
how to recognize love her
motionless there
when the need for her caress
still haunts us
so often so far away

95

the pleasure of the text
the pleasure of reading
to open the office of the title
with a knife
there to find Alechenski
like an officer of words

to come back on a pale Sunday
of a miserable winter's day
the light changing
there is no more horizon
no more country
only an enormous grey sky
the seemingly endless
January snow

Translated by D.G. Jones

ANDRÉ ROY

Saturday, at the Same Time

I'm far away as I watch you
and my very incomplete soul gives you
its permission to ignore the word "war"
and then as well the word "peace,"
my head is full of Slavic languages
and tattoos dancing,
nothing else but disorder.
You think you can speak love
with things stuck in your throat.

Tuesday Now Too Late

We all thought we invented God
but He had not given it a thought,
we, as solitary as the blue
on holiday in the night,
with our sleep held out at arm's length.
How many objects does infinity contain?

*

The true images will be the ones I'll weep over
when you're gone.
We won't speak any words
even when they pour from our mouths
unbidden.
Somewhere I know the Earth spins
        backwards.
Young man, read poetry
for the sake of metaphors remembered
which, one day, escaped the laws of gravity.
My past will not be a surprise to me when
        I touch you.

*

Each time I write someone loves me
for my interior things
laid to rest in the domain of tears;
I know one day the sky will be empty,
suddenly, like the images in a film
which have unrolled and trembled
for us, and then explode.
All that falls is probable;
the air like a public enemy.
I declare myself doomed because
        world-sick.

98

In the night that goes on and doesn't see us,
nothing else but an ocean of blood,
of adolescents fallen in all the wars,
I'm not weeping for myself but for the words
that condemn me as they leave me.
Certain that the truth is lying in every place,
even in the very dust of every room.
Young man, take up my thoughts without a cry,
listen to the music of the bees,
dance as if you were somewhere else.

*

God always kept quiet during wars.
Each day is the seventh one.
The sky moves but falls not.
Interior history is a chain of images,
here it is knotted in atomic reaches.
Beauteous beauty, has music always
            existed?
Sounds rising from the time of the Vanishing.
Young man, make enough movements to be seen,
so that desire flows quick and ready from your flesh
before the great conflagration.

Translated by Daniel Sloate

Denise Desautels

I count the days the letters
from the first word without a break
the distant voice turned aside
the voice changed by our own disorder
you fall back on resemblance.

then a place a desire unbearable
in the endless cities when memory falters
yet I see that mirrors and marshes
simply swallow what needs to be lost:
this habit of recalling the past.

then only indiscretion trips us up.

*

I write in the present.

the trip plagued with strange twists traps
you say the colours of September
distort the landscape, you say my voice
slips on the word, you say the way out
like a one-way street.
while I consider the question of silence
our bodies move on the giddy September.

we no longer know anything since we resist.

naturally we come back to it

photographs of the trip
shades of blue and green disposition
of a body a mouth there where the drama
calls for difference and delay:
what the body leaves incomplete
what happens to words after
the amorous commentary.

again I reply: writing doesn't take care of itself
    or its peril.

I'm saying what happened

and you are looking at the words sliding between
my teeth the words that break up the
movement of the sea between the teeth.

at night the angle of the wound
doesn't allow the story that concerns us
to escape nor the flash of death nor the arrousal nor
the voice modulating the countenance of bodies.
at night the moving sheets reinvent
the gestures when the voice is lost.

then I mumm passion as a simple story.

Translated by D.G. Jones

101

JEAN-PAUL DAOUST

New York

It's examining the sky
New York and its schizo-clinic
Burroughs and Mick Jagger *hand in hand*
Tom Waits weeps from Marilyn's eyes
Frozen in a mirror on Broadway
the *Chorus Lines* stretch out like an Egyptian panel
HAPPY BIRTHDAY MICKEY you save the Fifth
The last of the Andrews all in plastic
Is celebrating   in a *BLUE MINK JAZZ* at the *Backstage*
42nd Street and its parade of asses all dressed
                                        just for you honey
We're on the brink of insanity but we step back
                              we want to see the next
show
In Bloomingdale's I start searching for Rita Hayworth
Quite drunk and swinging my umbrella
I walk towards
the credit cards make *swish swish*
I love New York
the only city that doesn't sleep
Full of tunes the heart is smitten by a star
King Kong is french-kissing the statue of Liberty
the tourists Xerox themselves

just for THE fun
Attempts to poison the crocodiles in the sewers
                              were apparently successful

It's lovely it's warm and New York is undulating
                                        like a
cobra made of honey
Circles under my eyes right down to the mouth my tongue
                  made of lace my eyes *punk I*
WALK
Visions eclipsed by paranoid eyelashes
FROM *HAPPY HOUR TO HAPPY HOUR*
BROADWAY IS MY STYLE
my smile naively full of *sparkles*
So what
Why New York

Hollywood

The silence of a winter's evening
The door closed
The surroundings forgotten
Only a vista of snow
The frost of the hour
Full of the imaginary's flashes
Because in reality winter nights are black
Blacker than the others
Interminable
I write in the snow
Words of love that freeze
Words of solitude, pallid and stale
The winter pursues me right to the bones of my soul
That skin so cold on his blood so hot
Festivities are difficult in the cold
The windows look like telephones off the hook
Insane
To stare at so much white
Only this phantom pulse of life
Only an old silent film
I am a fallen star
With the Hollywood archives as her prison

103

Sunday Afternoon

Death came in on a fine Sunday afternoon
The unexpected heat of that early May
It was the day the child understood
the sun is of blood
The mother in mourning for love for life
The child the tragic fragrance of lilacs
Death is written in mauve
Lost epitaph make-up
On the father's death-mask see the shame
the fury
It's there in the family crypt slapped alphabet
Death inscribing in the flesh of the living
Sadness helplessness
The torture of that Sunday afternoon
May 5, 1957

*A poet remembers that on that day his father was gone for
good a child remembers a Sunday in May the loveliest month
in the calm waters sing the crystal sirens that bay as though
in the hollow of both hands on the verge of clasping together
the light bursting at the end of that unforgettable Sunday those
clouds the steeples pierce like dragons being eviscerated in the
waters the perch swim with flashes of gold but the child that
Death caresses with hands of ice*

The water flows into eternity
The child watches forbidden festivities
the loveliest sunset dismembered clouds
Pools of blood carnage of the gold
Death is the winner as everywhere else
On the water a ballet of metallic butterflies
the eyes the flames
And the fragrance of the lilacs drug him
Death spreads wings and tapers away
the bells continue to toll
On this Sunday afternoon opera
of the grief of the world
the father is dead spiralling echo
the child chased out of paradise

Translated by Daniel Sloate

CLAUDE BEAUSOLEIL

Prefatory

We must bear witness to our loss with grandeur
set out along the world's roads
leaving tracks that go only forward
through the burnt blackness of things
despite the whiteness that inhabits us
go far into hacked and butchered words
hoarse noises and strange concoctions of nothingness
we must foresee all name all
gather everything out of memory in the crumbling of
                                        our souls
in a rebirth with lightest siftings
between sentiments and cities
choose from among summits that scintillate with metals
by the precise beauty of injuries
when crystalline light knocks out windows along the
                                        horizon
diffusing hope in a song
so calm, so dense
and once more imaginable in the knowledge
that we must lose everything
plumb the abyss
dream without illusion yet without falling silent
go far and on and on
writing living loving
in infinite longing for the face of time

I'll Fly Away

I'll fly away
so the letters can form
these are the ideas that will cross space
and the text come back
wings stretched and calling
this is the magic street
of mirrors and vistas
this is the glance at games
in the hours' passion
this is the silence too that sometimes
is caught within us
this is often the rubbing away
and suddenly once more the rapture
but it's always this voice
always these accents
always these signs
these small objects of desire

106

I Saw Pink Flamingoes

for Nicole Smith

I saw pink flamingoes with coral wings
    and black feet
    their clear-cut colours straight
    from my childhood bathrooms
Their stylized flight
Through damp January air
    after a hurricane
When the freighted boat returns to the ruined wharf
    trailed by muddy water and mirages and time
Maybe I saw that maybe
I know
I believe in it
A colour of horizon
Which I invent
I see it
The ocean lower than the sands
The air damp
The storm
The dawning of the storm
And after
Abandonment
Beauty
I saw their wedge-shaped flight
The harmony
The boat sunk in sand
The sky pink
A memory from childhood
In a lost lagoon at the end of the Yucatan

107

Pure Picture of Poetry

A grief the grief of Nelligan
stirs me to think of fleeing
the fascination of poetry
reveals and proffers the absolute
like a backdrop for this city
glimpsed at the turning
by a park down a street
where the voice of his autumn poems
still floats
and his winter evenings born in us
to dream of loneliness
taking the heart as witness
to the beauty of his eyes
declaimed in poetry
the beauty of his hands
lifted to the light
in the city outlining
the glances of others
life utterly wears away
the truths of desire
whose unfurled mourning
at day's grey purlieu
teaches us to know
the completeness of solitude

Promise of Frost

So much sadness
compels me to recall
the evening's last words
in order to pronounce
an endless farewell
in the cold of no return
when January surprises
only winter's high winds
thresholds of the unbearable
given over to the secrets
of these waves of cold
when the crisp sounds of day
have no worth
every weapon is a blade
and murmurs are of glaciers
when I weep dumbfounded
at a story both living and dead
its soul in tatters
with the years, I know
and now wakened by the wind
in this winter that speaks
to me of the shiver
that is my heart my sister
in the only moment
when the gust brings me
the white whirl of nights
down empty sidewalks
where the epoch breaks off
at shores of ice
just so many years the less
where am I living where am I going
repeats the horizon

Translated by Judith Cowan

LUCIEN FRANCOEUR

The Tomb of Arthur Rimbaud

(for Heavy Metal Performance)

Oh, Rimbaud, my glorious punk
Like the Elvis of rictus and pelvis
Handsome Elvis on his wizard legs
And the one at the dance in St. Guy
On stage like you on all the highways
Oh Rimbaud of bohemian ways and the Green Café
My Rimbaud of the season in hell
Right to the end like Jim Morrison
Journey to the End of Night
This is the end

Rimbaud of kaleidoscopic vowels
Rimbaud of the hologrammatical word
Rimbaud of polychrome illuminations

Oh Rimbaud colored plates and laser-words
Rimbaud with the metallic blue gaze
Rimbaud with visions of Africa

Rimbaud of all rebellions
Of all deviancies
Of all clairvoyances

Rimbaud rocks on the walkman like Billy Idol
Rimbaud of city and jungle
Of the desert and the great escape

Rimbaud in a worn black Hell's Angels jacket
Rimbaud in torn blue skinhead jeans
Rimbaud like a rolling stone let it bleed
Rimbaud the exile on main street walking the dog
Rimbaud the street-fighting man born to be wild
Oh Rimbaud of the beggars' banquet
with your double-bladed switchblade words

Rimbaud with razor-blade visions
Rimbaud from everywhere as always
I shout your name into the conspiracy of time
I hear your black book on the ghetto-blasters

Your illuminashuns on nigger-boxes

Rimbaud heavy metal and satin tenderness at dawn
Rimbaud in prismacolour inside polyphonic vowels
Quadraphonic straight from the portable verb
Multiplex from integrated sonnets

Rimbaud long-life live in life
Being beauteous in cities

Rimbaud dharma bum and naked lunch
Rimbaud ill-at-ease and arrogant
Rimbaud with legs like Gene Vincent
Be-bop-a-lula rock'n'roll coochie coo
And with the juvenile fixation teenage lust
And the gaze of Johnny Rotten
White nigger of Ethiopia
and barbarian of the Hôtel Splendide

111

I write your name on the archways of forbidden cities
I write you name with a pocket knife on the walls of the
immeasurable

I inscribe your name with indelible ink on the skin of
humanity

The Next-To-Last Poem

Quadraphonic poetry
To the four corners of the universe
For the world or for humanity?

Within the fonts of the machine
Poetry lies in chips:
Computerized hieroglyphs.

Cracks, fissures, gaps
—Cathode clefts—

Timeworn ballpoints,
Dried-out markers,
Amazed fountain pens,

And if I were to write the last epidermic poem?

Translated by Hugh Hazelton

NORMAND DE BELLEFEUILLE

1. With Each Leg, the Unforeseeable Swerve

The dance does not take steps to respond. Step by step. The dance is not a science of response, no more than the misstep that yet carries the day.

Above all, the action that really unfolds—as an occasion of happiness, for because of it, though not a response, the real becomes tolerable, tolerable to the point even of provoking the desire for a response, of favouring the real with a richer countenance, deeper shadows, unheard-of angles, of favouring it with a Theory, however provisional, as to the real stakes put into play with each step, with each misstep that yet carries the day, with each tumble already slight and corrected by each leg each time reinvented under the body that falls, brutal and categoric—does not take steps to respond, step by step, is not a science of response.

The dance I imagine is not a matter of numbers or codes, related to god or faith or the son or a happy death; rather to the quick quiz and the unforeseeable swerve; for the dance I imagine certainly does not take steps to respond, for the dance I imagine is not a science of response.

2. The Dance Deals with the Adverbs

When suddenly the dance gives the adverbs a holiday. When
there are only four memories which correspond to each
recreated angle of the arm, the hip almost disjointed, the wing
and the eyelash which fluttering signifies: "four memories in
each corner when the head is in play"—then against boredom
the dance suddenly gives the adverbs a holiday, steps out,
closes up, beats with a cupped hand and a hollow sound steps
out and closes up beats with a cupped hand and a hollow sound
which resembles the cough of the monsters mornings with so
much drink mornings with so much declamatory talk
mornings with so much hope despite murder and madness.

When there are only four memories at each corner when the
head is in play—for it will no longer be a question of death,
much less the condition of the heart: to begin with there were
the thick soups and the pepper, the vanilla ice-cream sodas, the
well-groomed uncles then the mother who dances, giving the
adverbs a holiday with each re-created angle of her arm, of
her hip almost disjointed.

114

Other figures as well, but mornings, before the drink, before
the hope, these are already quite enough for me to love.

Translated by D.G. Jones

Denis Vanier

HANDICAPPED
STOP CARING FOR YOURSELVES
THE TRACES
OF YOUR ELBOWS IN THE SAND
ARE ITS LAST
VESTIGE OF SHELLIFE

115

Dream

My greatest dream was to never have one.
Putting aside most nightmares which only
oscillate between fear and desire—though such evidence
can only prove the insatiable rapport between
the police and the strict sexuality
of the extreme right.

Such sad texts, I don't believe I've ever
written any
except those that well eloquently from vessels
without carrying power.

I've never dreamed, except about you
to fuck you or to kill you.

Outside Sentences of Death

we tell the beads of exterior life
at the very moment when night
can no longer recover from discharging
in its arms
more touching than the wet tramplings
moose of sweet relief
all gathered at the display of oppression
with the sign as trap
in these pages of the bible of wounds
shooting themselves with drugs
which is an impediment to crime
but simple and helpful
nevertheless he keeps his straps under his arm
had it not been for the lack of an inkpot
he'd have ordered a federal curretage
of his immensity

117

Evil

Let it tip, spill, this warm oil
on your linen sheets
under the mess of soaked woolens

Everything's got to be burned
    blank out her memory
    in the vinegar of space

    kill your sister
cover her with oysters and honey

    There's no ointment can soothe
not even total effacement
it's with that however
one washes one's hair
after the commotion

something doesn't sprout any more
where the stains are, wet spicy tea

    a hollow button
to press in case of emergency
reminding us intimacy
is the property of others

my face slowly crumbles
my skin floats in the air
we attend the swelling
of the white tumor under the eye

even afterwards I no longer remember
how one dies

before at least I found it painful enough
to be reminded

YOLANDE VILLEMAIRE

from *Quartz and Mica*

The setting sun washes the trees in Central Park with pink light
I stand at the window with a Perrier in my hand
our Delegate General moves graciously among her guests
as we celebrate Québec's *Fête nationale* at the New York Athletic Club
a guest musician plays Claude Champagne's *Suite villageoise*
and balloons with *fleurs-de-lys* on them float across the ceiling
a designer wearing red spectacles tells me about a *Fête de la Saint-Jean*
in Los Angeles
the buildings of the Upper East Side stand out against the pastel sky
I wish I could feel moved but this is not moving

*

Now we are alone on the beach in the wind
he says to me "je t'aime" in French
New York recedes to thousands of light-years away
I can feel his heart beating through his hand
and I weep with joy
as tenderly he strokes my hair
the spirit of the wind whispers in my ear
the evil spirit is breathing madness to me
I pray to heaven to let me love

119

*

I am translating the black box of a craft that came from Ursa Major
can talmac yinko hobike ugh om ulak lock
I am an oceanographer and a linguist
I have just come from the Mendeleev Centre for Deprogramming
and I hurt my ankle during teletransport
on my breasts I can still feel the hands of the stranger
I ask him if he can remember having lived before this life
he says he remembers that I was a scientist
that he was assigned to deprogram me and that he loved me

Young Woman, Red

I would have liked to meet him
on a sunny day
walking hatless through a park
those were the days when my hair was bright red
from a distance, he hadn't recognized me
standing at the water's edge
and watching the play of shadows
I smiled at him
without speaking he came closer
and then we talked
and laughed
there were a lot of yellow butterflies
the wind was soft
it was sunny and warm
where were you then?
can talmac yinko hobike ugh om ulak lock
I am an imagining woman
we are in darkness
I declare that the time has come
I am writing a book that will be a machine
to open our reality

Translated by Judith Cowan

JOSÉE YVON

"No Coach Will Ever Tell Me What to Do!"

Bike-riding girl
pain-in-the-neck girl
yeah—I root myself
in difficulty.

She who needed to be lost
cleaned the ashtrays
reached the end of her glory.

If you weren't too thirsty
you'd understand
star of this morsel of a life
star of this morsel of a dream
eh why not *let's go get drunk tonight*"

"everybody has to lose a day"
fragment of a life
fragment of a dream
what are you doing

121

Caress

my cracked fingers caress you once again
with the greenish oil of a barium feast
to provide the necessary pieces
an eyeful of white
a thousand tiny balloons in the brain
and throbbing pectorals
one's inflated insinuation
toward the destruction of all free radicals

for the agony of a people
in the Fucketeria,
the eye of the storm
and you goddess of the taiga
in the dance of sick dervishes
you've gone pale
something out of character for you

Alone

yes I take root in difficulty
wear a scab
a sickly green electric kind of bodice
an ass's skin
anywhere between the cement where I take root
no very profound tenderness
to this underhanded sickness
in losing the blanket of response
under the pillow of blue lights
that reduces the arrival into this world
of each naive girl with too-traditional dreams
since I'm all alone on the scene

Translated by Sonja Skarstedt

ROGER DES ROCHES

Reality

1.

Reality:
as if one discovered the mechanics of looking
were linked to those of fleeing.
In the landscape
as if the trees stood firm,
but the passersby, no.
Then, in the sky molded to this landscape,
pierced from behind, unstarred,
as if something that was always flying was
always retreating.

Or rather:
covered over with snow, with footprints;
the rain that sweeps over it
releases odours and voices.

124

2.

The snow like milk;
the sidewalks like bread.
I presume what's coming toward me,
whirled by the wind,
will shortly be lost
in what I've left behind.
That's the order, though not so quick.
Afterwards it matters little if it's me who's breathing:
the smoke comes out of my mouth;
the real world, out of the mouths of others.

If I come home from work, I'm too cold,
I write short novels.

I've brought nothing with me to measure
the yellow interior of houses.

There's but one truth: yours, then mine.

3.

The rhythm, the river, the sequence of steps,
the gaze turned on one's self,
each step toward the river that runs in one direction
    and the other.
As if one were born often
almost always in the same way;
painlessly, will-lessly, aimlessly.

One is born each time, as usual, one lights
    another cigarette.

4.

OPERATION reading; OPERATION becoming.
A few centimetres from the earth, its soul.
Each tree, an opening in the sky:
the marvellous hand that keeps its grip on a direction.

Stirring the water that waits.
OPERATION walking:
impossible without the help of the past.

The poem will collect itself little by little
in the poems I didn't think I'd written.

Translated by D.G. Jones

YVES BOISVERT

Changing Places

FIRST

     Eternity grows in open fields.

SECOND

     An entire Canada goose of distress
          looks back in flight.

LAST

     You are leaving just the same for Cap d'Espoir
     you are choosing the alienation of the sea.

Ordinary Poem

It's all been shattered by a blow that was a long time coming
      it's true chains can be heard clanking from far off
it's true it cracks bones   empties stomachs
like nothing else

it took up the street as it would have the sea
it's true it wasn't even as old as the birds
barely more than two hands two feet two times

it broke its neck its back
it was shared among all of us
it's nothing it cries and it's gone
sometimes
like nothing else
it trips over the brooch
with a knife between its lips
in shirt-tails in winter

it tears itself from all the wharves
      leaves the beseiged ports
      sings once it gets beyond
      shines in the middle of the night
      speaks the silence of beasts
      bleats to death at wolves the moon
      and sleeps in the stars

it's all been shattered
it costs an arm and a leg.

At School

At school
they were told
that the world was badly made.
They resolved
not to add anything to it.

At school
they were told
that life was fake.
They decided to lie.

At school
they were told
that everything was the same.
They judged
the acceptable as equal to the unacceptable.

At school
they were told
that war was global
and that everything would soon be over
and they said yes
let's finish it off once and for all.

The Return

The weather's not always good
but there are a lot of them there
faces blackened hard-working and tired
driven by bells
and you among them all are
so sweet   so beautiful   so calm.

The weather's not always good
and without my looking for you
I see you coming
and you come to me when night is falling
the day is at its height night falls
and you recross the path of all the others

every time the birds look at you
every time the birds fly away
you come to me in that same black dress
and your face is paler than any paleness.

The weather's not always good
so I open my biggest door
and you invade the space
children become flustered all around
and we stay silent
as I press close against your falling white warmth.

Sail

A sail should never be judged too quickly
by its cloth   its form   its force
you can't always tell the limits
of freedom.

No one knows what nerves are made of
nor what dawn will tear us from our skin
of servitude
You can't know the silk you weave
nor the boats you repair
nor the wild beasts of the ocean you touch
with breath
nor the miniscule lakes where people drown themselves.

You can't tell the barkings of the rivers
without kennels or traps or collars
or the desire that fills the canvas
and gives the wind its fury
to invent its force its form
and its new-found solitude.

Translated by Hugh Hazelton

Jean-Marc Desgent

You've got Someone in Your Arms

You've got someone in your arms I recognize
Will he lose his life through every orifice?
Matter, let's melt it down between us.
Your voice modulates the rhythm of the real.
The rain, it's really pouring now.
I am there, all around you.
Push the curtain and look at me.
Grasp me bodily.
Let me invent your provenance
and the desire to tell you non-stop:
the botany, every zoology of my childhood,
space and my astrological chart.
You cheat with your last toss of the dice.
You are born in stages, one after another.
I go on, straying in pleasure,
to damp the human fire.
We run to to get to the sea.
You drag me along hanging on your lips.
You've got the idea of playing in seaweed.
Look at me anew to see if I am.

131

You're Talking in the Line of Fire

You're talking in the line of fire,
this flash and ravishment of blue light
this vital blue flash,
to indicate clearly the fury,
the dash of your eyes,
the acute angle of your gaze.
You're talking out of the beyond,
whirlwind or drift,
of this tireless will to spring into view.
You're talking of your flesh coating words,
You're hanging out in the inner world:
with long veils,
with the beautiful colours
of trees, of lichen, brushed up
in the space of my head.
You're passing your bodies over my pupils.
You're navigating, rounding the unknown,
the distress, the impatience of the sea.
It's there now I say my name.
You are the ambivalence of things.
Caress me with the back of your hand.
Deliver me of all that I carry.
You stroll at the crossing of bodies and ideas:
there, blind gods meet each other
there, halt gods kill each other,
there, demented gods mime our lives.
You're wearing your hair in knots,
also, however, your hair's standing on end.
You are the ambivalence of things.

This enigma delights me.
You're talking right in my ear:
undulation of your song.
The voice, endless voice.
Are you coming to look for me?
I'm writing to you in order to be loved.

Translated by D.G. Jones

132

FRANÇOIS CHARRON

The Beauty of Faces Does not Weigh on the Earth

my soul goes out to the centre of calm even as the fields
        grow more busy again
the birds getting ready to go south
I remain with you, it is seven-thirty
our quick eyes offer no resistance to the fragility
        of the evening
filtered by a window we hear the sound of water
our shadow precedes us, you show me a green
        apple
we are about to touch the first person who comes

                    *

I hang around until the first shadows appear without
        asking myself why
it must be nine o'clock in the evening
your eyes sparkling in a burst of laughter
a light comes on in a car
we get nearer each other in order to hug
        each other
it is slightly less cold than yesterday

I work late before going to bed
this morning two women had to run not to miss
        the last bus
the weather is mauve, I feel I've no particular
        recollections of the past
a man casts a quick glance at his hat while passing
        a storefront
words I've picked up have no affect
I light up my second cigarette
the truth is every moment we come down to earth

133

I caress the candour of your breasts
your eyelids lower, the visible no longer carries
      the same sense
the dates die on the calendar without dying
a corner of the rug lights up in the sun
we are listening to what has never been
      for the first time
we are this childhood unfamiliar to us
we are fresh as the finest drizzle that has
      fallen on things

unfolded it is our imagination colours
      the deserted village
summer comes to a close
a spider scurries to take refuge under a dresser
I've recognized you in an old photograph
you look at me insistently and at the same time
      a cloud hides the sun
evening gets lost over the bed
speech is not indispensable

      *

I hum a bit of music in my head
the cold goes right through the fabric of my coat
in the clockface there is a large black hand
the blinds are down, memory seems unreal
somewhere, a nameless country burns endlessly
air dreams us, air fulfills us
they seem one, the feeling of loving and dazzled death
which I can see

Translated by D.G. Jones

RENAUD LONGCHAMPS

Decimations

May earthly time pass
and we return
to eternity

It's one beast devouring the other
space and necessity

Of my body I've wished the loss
of the least particle

In the heavy nature of our tears
the ocean is stirred up,
evaporates

At night
I sleep beneath the scales, ancestral,
of the first birds

135

I belong to eternity

You can look after the time of death
and impossible matter
subject to constraint
subject to nature never touched

Don't add any more of this blue
to the heavens

For you belong to the order
that nourishes chaos
with stars
and simian polymaths

I will walk toward the tired light
without waiting for the universe,
future black hole

I will walk in footsteps
invisible
to space and time

Mine is the chalky solitude
of the primal cry

Between the schists and the clay
the sky withdraws,
tributary of air and water

The species crosses itself
and falters on the bivouac

The predator cocks an ear
closes its jaws, again

There it is, the finishing touch
without restraint
without memory

You go rushing down this hill
looking for the wind
raising
the cry

You flee
and you come back

In your heart an eventual black hole

Translated by D.G. Jones

LOUIS JACOB

Keys

On the day's horizon the
quotidian knocks on the door
like an excess of every day
with a thousand times over the same
hands, the same jobs

deep in the eyes of the evening
a light blinks on and off persistent
as an excess of dials
as a thousand times over the same
waiting, the same questions

deep in somebody's body
with a thousand times over the same efforts
the same hope meant to mean
a child's come to the door of the world
and turns the knob

Common Poem

(for friends in common)

evening empties its drawers
in thin-lipped souvenir city
behind you memories return
the ink dreams in your old books

noises are filtering out
from the sleep of the inner cities
those of misery that walks back to front
in its attachment to its paddies
not to end like a sidewalk on the street

the walls of your room no sky
stick to your skin
and you lend an ear to the alleys

your stomach rushes round in its toes
the weight of mountains on your lids
all the salt of the sea in the harbour
so many down years in your look
you keep an eye half cocked
on the turn of the locks

day by day your *fin de siècle*
arrives then dawn
breaking red
starts balancing the moons lost
in the scales of time

while under the city's clocks
beyond the algorithms of know-how
clowns in suits a bit bushed stop going round
before getting caught up by the neck
in the balance of a world to be done

139

The Timetable

Dawn's dunked in a cup
coffee complicates
the step towards the door
outside a few spikes of morning breath
and the hour is head over heels with its workers

evening is smoking plates
raw meat has teeth
followed by a few beers of evening breath
then the step towards the hourly beds
and its workers head over heels with the night

love's metronome, work's
make the good times and the bad times pass
in the end memory rests on its appetite
somewhere in childhood
then night and the hour creak a bit more
and life too without its workers

Translated by D.G. Jones

Marie Uguay

In metamorphosis, the city is launched
into the white brocade of winter
or the magic glass of its skyscrapers
(Behind a window the relaxed
back of a rush chair evokes
the happy weaving of
some excursion or other in the sun)

In the dark the birch tree is an amorous sign
a divisible river and waiting
its candour seems to cleave a lucid night

Of all the days and all the sick nights
I've kept only the harrassment of my love
only this monotonous destruction of the sky
only this slow extinction of my senses
I no longer recognize my body
I've entered an awkward universe informed
solely by the trepidation of the streets

141

Still, they exist, apples and oranges
Cézanne holding in one hand
all the fecund amplitude of earth
the vigorous beauty of fruit
I do not know every fruit by heart
nor the restorative warmth of fruit on a white sheet

But hospitals are endless
factories are endless
line-ups in the freezing cold are endless
beaches turned into swamps are endless

I've known those who suffer to their last gasp
and whose dying is endless
listening to the sound of a violin or that of a crow
or that of the maples in spring

Endless their drive to reach the rivers within
that carry in their flood floes of light
shreds of the seasons   they have so many dreams

But the barriers   the waiting-rooms are endless
Tortures   cancers are endless
men who struggle in the mines
amid the roots of their people
who are mowed down point blank   leaping from the
                                        fray
endlessly dreaming
the colour orange

Women endlessly sewing up men
and men pouring themselves a drink

Still, despite the ever increasing furrows in the face of
                                        the world
despite the ever increasing number of exiles
the wounds again and again
inflicted in the blindness of stones
I snare, still, the sound of the waves
the peacefulness of oranges

Gently, Cézanne, in his composition, appeals
                        to the suffering of the earth
and the whole dynamic summer comes to rouse me
comes gently   desperately to bequeath me its fruit

142

The window's a screen
on which lives pass
under the gestation of the snows
the reverberations of torpor
Depthless canvas of showers
the window traces the obverse of your face
Stretched
an oil   a sketch   a film
Geometry of fields and of weathers
Garden
Shop window
The whole universe has remained on the other side of
                                        the gaze

Having gone through the window
the eye, the pupil, forgets
shattering and shards
we have entered into matter
into the quicksilver of the subject
into history
We have tasted, finally, faces and things

Translated by D.G. Jones

Bernard Pozier

Seven-year-old Rockers

they leave for school still half asleep
nudging and shoving impatiently
until at last the three o'clock bell
rings to release them back to life

ceremoniously
they lace their running shoes
slip on their jeans
and t-shirt screens
that project their idols in the eyes of passers-by

felt pens do for their tattoos
E.T. stickers make great badges
and the roles they play
so seriously
make dreamy wrinkled frowns
on the barbarous brows of their tender years

they prowl the sidewalks adventure-prone
nervy, skittish and vain
scarring the pavement as they go
with wheely squeals
of their intersidereal
minibikes

proud as peacocks
strong as titans
at the slightest slight
from their little chums
at their trifling feats
or at daring to say "shit"

and then they burst into the house
like so many riffs on the guitar
put on their discs of rhythmic tunes
they mimic as much as dance to

144

they stock up on posters and magazines
the ones that feature the singers they know
play the Rolling Stones for their birthday songs
burning some laps of their bright brief years

they're right at home electronic-wise
and care little for bumps
when they play robot

eyes on the alert
lips curled back
ears cocked
hair like a battlefield
when you've lost the fight

as pure as heroes of comic strips
their heads in the stars
always ready to scrap
to find mountainous molehills everywhere

between the fictions that they live
and reality that invents their lives
between the planks of the backyard fence

and under the counter of life
these little gypsy-hearted kids
pass the contraband
of their great discoveries
and their tiny emotions

scruffy and scratched
they leave like scouts
trail-blazing the land of to be
with resplendent smiles

but never know that at their turf's end
at the street corner they never turn
at the frontier of what's not allowed
where suddenly you're grown up
Nothing
awaits them
little seven-year-old rockers

The Real Thing

all alone on the neighbourhood rink
blades planted firmly on the ice
seeing himself a champion
yet another little kid
set free in the wooden pen
waiting for a phantom pass
to slam into the waiting goal
to score the world's most important point
in his wish-fulfilling dream
jamming the puck into the net
and tumbling after
with a little shout of real joy
in a puff of cold smoke
he lifts his arms toward the sky
toward the stars

Translated by Philip Stratford

146

ÉLISE TURCOTTE

In the Delta of the Night

Night flight.

Speaking is displaced. Across the night I see that I'm
seated in the moon of the spotlight; I'm wearing a long
black boa and I'm playing the bass violin. It's lovely.
Then the words go adrift flake away echolalia of
skeletons I think neuter cancelled in places unbearable
cascades alcohol of torrential rains in the wings to
recover the decor which is falling I am speaking I am
speaking of the dizziness silence cleaving the distance
the singular distance all the time wanting to get away
from the qui-vive of words exact willed asking where is
the exit of this theatre in flames it is hot scraping of pop
corn ice cream soda lost the light the exit. One must
keep an eye on oneself or run in the streets, at risk,
burning to know oneself.

*

Lips in the fingers. Hair.

You'd like to suppress all points of reference sticking
to a new skin each time. But you get involved in a
whole tangle of memories. Of lives. You call up some
thing. Shadowy.

Voice.

I say your name, on bridges, in town. You come into the
room, say my name with another voice.

Warships

The first day, I was bent on looking at what did not yet
exist like a warship motionless on a dead sea. A single
survivor was tirelessly singing, always the same song,
for fear of losing her voice, her tiny voice grown faint
in the noonday sun. On the table there was a terrible
jigsaw puzzle whose pieces I was furiously trying to put
together. I knew I was going to live in another house.
In my dream bodies moved, groped in the dark, circled
round a stage, a fragile stage, so very fragile, in the
depth of the silence.

*

The door is glass-paned. Her middy is barely
reflected in it as on some worn image. A hasty sketch.
On the table, a postcard where it's written I love you.
Suddenly she notices the ship then the deck where
I'm sleeping in a half swoon. The emotion of infinite
blue, she's lost in it as in some oversize outfit. She's
watching me, blissfully ignorant, to see what I retain of
her, what about her called forth the swoon. The heart
pounding the wake.

Translated by D.G. Jones

148

HÉLÈNE DORION

Time's Corridors

You are no longer entirely there
you disappear
slowly in me
time no longer means life

*

My death will be like
all others
that upset and leave indifferent
because too far at times

*

The colour inscription, that day:
twenty-nine years well written.

I do not forget that the day before
you had torn from me the emotion
of loving you I do not forget
these words—I will come
perhaps perhaps not

149

The corner of the street is nothing
but another street-corner
since you stopped appearing there
to join me

The earth still turns
without you
the sun rises
scours the bones
and life comes back charging

*

You hold out your hand
towards me who would like to take it
so far away that nothing would exist
in this hand but mine

I am searching for the gesture that will be a path.

I would have asked you how
and where life goes
in you
if I could have held back the line
that cut

Translated by Andrea Moorhead

SERGE PATRICE THIBODEAU

The Passage of Ice Fields

and I would be asleep so you would never know
because I keep quiet and conceal even a hint of
my choice
and no one ever approaches me
because the wounds are raw and open to the sun
which falls on them and sets me on fire and grabs hold of
my body
so lucid that one day it makes a mistake
and strays
and leaps to the ground and that stops everything
sand in the mouth.

*

and if you told me that the dance had resumed
that the sudden revivals were calculated
for each and every one of us
if you told me your faith in life
and your inadequacy confronted with the man
eroded
humiliated by so many illusions, so much erosion
if you were to erase the bitterness and extravagance in me
would I dare perhaps believe you
if you told me then that everything was over.

151

We, The Stranger

silty the shores withdraw from each other
nothing prevents me from leaving
all rivers lead to life
the summits fall there short of breath

lusting afer running away enthusiasm emerges
steep
tawny and yet so fluid against the shoulder
and its lip sticky

will I be given a day to imitate these books'
transparence and radiance
to free with my entire body the musky odour
of worn leather bindings
my gaze clothed in gold powder and my speech bare?
the mirror's vanity devours itself
opaque wing against time's acrid flame

I will need as an asset a wound
silent
and from the foam
of the pebbles and broken oars of my past
we are young
at our windows all the murderous anxieties
break

and the day rises already fixed the wait set
by the calendar
like a phase of the moon
like ground the blade butchers

we speak the introspective language of clay
under bridges
of buckwheat's redness in autumn
of the horizon distinct against the brightness

and if I claim your presence
it's so I can better abandon your flesh

the love between us occupies its place
between us
and brushes neither against your body nor my palm
silty the shores withdraw from each other
nothing prevents me from leaving

Translated by Andrea Moorhead

BIOGRAPHICAL NOTES

Rina Lasnier (1910): Born in Saint-Grégoire-d'Iberville, the author as well of dramatic texts on Biblical themes, she has received many awards, including the Prix David (1974). A prolific and profound writer, her work, characterized by a demanding and finely honed sense of language, and inspired by a mystical conception of the world, has been collected in *Poèmes I* and *II* (Fides) and *L'ombre jetée I* and *II* (Écrits des Forges). Other translations in English can be found in *Ellipse,* No. 22 and No. 49.

Clément Marchand (1912): Born in Sainte-Geneviève-de-Batiscan, he was early associated with the weekly paper and publishing house, *Bien public*. His collection, *Les soirs rouges,* won the Prix David (1939) and was a seminal work in presenting an urban and humanist approach to poetry.

Anne Hébert (1916): Born in Sainte-Catherine-de-Fossambault, a cousin of Saint-Denys-Garneau, she has also written plays, short stories, and novels, some of which have been made into films. Widely celebrated, her poetry captures the essence of her whole oeuvre and finds its fullest expression in the collections *Les songes en equilibre, Le tombeau des rois, Mystère de la parole,* and *Le jour n'a d'égal que la nuit.* Of the various English translations of her work, the most recent is *Anne Hébert: Selected Poems,* tr. Al Poulin (Stoddart).

Alphonse Piché (1917): Born in Chicoutimi, he has lived most of his life in Trois-Rivières, at the confluence of the Saint Lawrence and Saint Maurice Rivers, excellent for boating and an inspiration in his work. He also celebrates the lives of ordinary people in *Ballades de la petite extrace.* His more recent poetry focusses bluntly on the pains and declining powers of old age and the approach of death. Some translations in English can be found in *Ellipse,* No. 47.

Gilles Hénault (1920): Born in Saint-Majorique, he grew up in Montreal. A journalist and art-critic, he co-founded the publishing house, *Cahiers de la file indienne.* His poetry has been collected in *Signaux pour les voyants.* Other English translations can be found in *Ellipse,* No. 18.

Gaston Miron (1928): Born in Saint-Agathe-des-Monts, he has become a kind of ambassador par excellence of Quebec poetry around the world. One of the founders of the publishing house L'Hexagone, he has long been active as an animator, as a link between several generations, and as a spokesman, both for poetry and an independent Quebec. His collection, *L'homme rapaillé,* is one of the most widely read and frequently translated texts of all Quebec literature. English translations can be found in D.G. Jones and Marc Plourde, tr. *Embers and Earth* (1984) and D.G. Jones, ed. *The March to Love: Selected Poems* (1986).

Gilles Vigneault (1928): Born in Natashquan, one of Quebec's greatest popular singers, he is also one of the masters of formal verse in this century. Co-founder of the review *Émourie* and founder of the publishing house Arc, he has devoted himself equally to poetry and song writing since the fifties. Of poems gathered in *Silences,* many rival, in their exemplary language and form, the songs of *Le grand cerf volant.*

Roland Giguère (1929): Born in Montreal, a painter, engraver and editor, he is one of the great Quebec Surrealists. The founder of Erta, he specializes in limited editions, combining print and prints, and has published a number of major Quebec poets. His poems have been largely collected in *L'Âge de la parole, La main au feu,* and *Forêt vierge folle.* English translations can be found in Donald Winkler,tr., *Rose & Thorn: Selected Poems of Roland Giguère* (Exile Editions).

Paul-Marie Lapointe (1929): Born in Saint-Félicien, drawing heavily on Surrealism and the world of jazz, he first published *Le vierge incendié,* one of the beacons of contemporary Quebec poetry. A journalist, for many years in the news department of Radio Canada, he has been widely translated and has received an award from the International Poetry Forum in Pittsburgh. However, one must add the monumental *Ecriture,* whose extreme linguistic play is full of surprises and tests the limits of the intelligible. Selected English translations are available in Lapointe, *The Terror of the Snows* and *The Fifth Season.,* tr. D.G. Jones (Exile Editions).

Janou Saint-Denis (1930): Born in Montreal, she has acted in radio and television, later on the stage. First in Paris, then in Montreal, she has organized various public readings of poetry, creating *"Place aux poètes."* Her main collections are *La roue de feu sceret* and *Mémoire innée.*

Denise Boucher (1935): Born in Victoriaville, she has worked primarily as a journalist, but also as a song-writer for such singers as Pauline Julien, Louise Forestier, Gerrry Boulet, and Dan Bigras. In theater, she has given us *Les fées ont soif,* a classic of feminist drama in Quebec; in poetry, *Cyprine, Paris polaroïd, Grandeur nature,* and *À coeur du jour.*

155

Suzanne Paradis (1936): Born in Quebec City, a novelist and literary critic, she has published some fifteen collections of poetry, including *La Malebête* (which won the *Prix de la province de Québec*), *L'oeuvre de pierre, Pour voir les plectrophanes naître, Les chevaux de verre,* and *Un goût de sel* (winner of the Governor General's Award for Poetry.)

Yves Préfontaine (1937): Born in Montreal, anthropologist and sociologist, amateur of jazz and civil servant, a strong supporter of the independence of Quebec, much of his poetry has been collected under the title *Parole tenue.* A cultivated man, a piano player, active in radio, he particularly shines in public readings of poetry. Translations in English can be found in Préfontaine, *This Desert Now,* tr. Judith Cowan (Guernica).

Gérald Godin (1938-1994): Born in Three Rivers, he worked as a journalist, was elected to the National Assembly, and became a minister in the Partis québécois government. He also directed *Québec-Presse* and the Publishing House Partis Pris. He defended the ordinary citizen, including many immigrants in his Montreal riding, was passionate about French and became a master of the vernacular. Mixing the resources of formal and colloquial language, he created a poetry with a unique voice, pungent and lively. Most of his poems have been collected in *Ils ne demandaient qu'à brûler.* After a long struggle, he finally succumbed to a brain tumour. For translations into English, see Godin, *Evenings at Loose Ends,* tr. Judith Cowan (Véhicule).

Madeleine Gagnon (1938): Born in Amqui, a university professor and a member of *l'Académie des lettres du Québec,* politically engaged as a québécoise and as a feminist, she has worked closely with Denise Boucher, Hélène Cixous, Annie Leclerc and Annie Cohen. Her early work has been collected in *Autographie I.* Later publications include *Au coeur de la lettre, Pensées du poème, Les fleurs du Catalpa, L'infante immémoriale,* and *Chant pour un Québec lointain.* For translations in English, see *Ellipse,* No. 33/34—also *Lair* and *Song for a Far Quebec* (Coach House Press).

Jean Royer (1938): Born in Saint-Charles-de-Bellechasse, historian, critic and anthologist of Quebec poetry, he aso founded the review *Estuaire.* His selected *Poèmes d'amour* received the *Prix du Journal de Montréal* and the *Prix Claude-Sernet.* He is literary director of l'Hexagone, and secretary of l'Académie des lettres du Québec.

Paul Chamberland (1939): Born in Longueuil, he became a co-founder of the review *Partis Pris* and, beginning with *Terre Québec* and *L'afficheur hurle,* he spoke to a number of different developments within Quebec poetry, from the more extreme expression of the counter-culture to a more philosophical, then global and clearly utopian, writing leading to his present *Géogrammes.* He now teaches creative writing at *l'Université de Québec à Montréal.* For English translations from *L'afficheur hurle* see Malcolm Reid, *The Shouting Sign Painters.*

Gilbert Langevin (1939-1995): Born in La Dorée, he produced a series of ironic sketches, in prose and verse, under the pseudonym, Zéro Legel. He also wrote songs for such singers as Pauline Julien, Marjo, Pierre Flynn, Offenbach, and Dan Bigras. Mixing tenderness and protest, he published a number of collections of poems, notably *Ouvrir le feu, Griefs, Mon refuge est un volcan,* and *Comme un lexique des abîmes.* For a selection of his poems in English translation, see the bilingual edition, *Body of Night* (Guernica), edited and translated by Marc Plourde.

156

Pierre Chatillon (1939): Born in Nicolet, he has also published novels and short fiction whose imagery constitutes a lyric celebration of life. Much of his poetry has been collected in *Poèmes (1956-1982).* Among recent collections, one may note *L'arbre des mots, Le violon soleil,* and *L'ombre d'or.* Among other awards, he has received the *Prix de la ville de Trois-Rivières,* where he is a university professor.

Michel Beaulieu (1941-1985): Born in Montreal, he was a prolific poet and also an editor, an animator, and a critic. His poetry explores the day to day detail of life in the cities and is informed by a signal tenderness. It has been collected primarily in two volumes, *Desseins* and *Indicatif Présent (et d'autres poèmes).* For a selection of his poems translated into English, see *Ellipse,* No. 36 and Arlette Francière, tr., *Spells of Fury* and *Perils of a Solemn Body* (Exile Editions).

France Theoret (1942): Born in Montreal, early a member of the editorial board of *la Barre du Jour,* she helped to create both the feminist review *Les têtes de pioche,* and the critical review *Spirale.* Her early work is collected in the Typo Edition of *Bloody Mary.* Her writing continues to explore the boundary between poetry and prose, reflection and lyric.

Pierre Morency (1942): Born in Lauzon, he has worked in radio, participated in the creation of the review *Estuaire,* and produced an eloquent book on the birds of Quebec and of other parts of the world. His singular work, drawing on a continental reality, has earned a number of awards, and includes such titles as *Au nord constamment de l'amour, Torrentials, Effets personnels* and *Quand nous serons.*

Nicole Brossard (1943): Born in Montreal, she has come to represent the leading edge of the formalist and feminist movements of Quebec writing. Prolific and varied, her writing has won a variety of awards and provoked a variety of translations. A selection of texts appears in *Ellipse*, No. 53 . She has also edited, with Lisette Girouard, the significant *Anthologie de la poésie des femmes au Québec.*

Francine Déry (1943): Born in Three Rivers, she has worked in the publishing business, and has herself published a number of books such as *En beau fusil, Le tremplin, Un train Bulgare,* and *Les territoires de l'excès,* evocative of the rage of desire.

Célyne Fortin (1943): Born in La Sarre, a painter and a co-founder of *Èditions du Noroît,* she has published various collections, including *Femme fragmentée, L'ombre des cibles, D'elles en elles,* and *Les intrusions de l'oeil.*

André Roy (1944): Born in Montreal, professor and film critic, he has published most of his work with Herbes Rouges. Primarily formal explorations of writing have been followed by a concern to describe the various stages of what he calls "the cycle of the passions." His collection *L'accélérateur d'intensité* has been reprinted in pocketbook format.

Denise Desautels (1945): Born in Montreal, she has published some twenty volumes, including *La promeneuse et l'oiseau, Mais la menace est une belle extravagance, Leçons de Venise,* and *Saut de l'ange.* Working close to the prose journal and meditation, frequently focussing on works of art, her distinctive writing has received a number of awards.

Jean-Paul Daoust (1946): Born in Valleyfield, a number of his earlier poems are collected in *Taxi pour Babylone.* His collection, *Les cendres bleues,* won the Governor General's Award for Poetry, and it is also available on cassette. He is the editor of the poetry magazine *Estuaire.*

157

Claude Beausoleil (1948): Born in Montreal, since 1970 he has published a variety of articles in newspapers and reviews and longer essays. He has brought out new editions of classic poets from Quebec as well as from foreign countries, and he has edited anthologies of foreign poets. He also puts out the review *lèvres urbaines.* He is a generous and prolific writer, whose work includes *Au milieu du corps l'attraction s'insinue, D'autres sourires des stars, Une certaine fin de siècle, S'inscrit sous le ciel gris en graphiques de feu, Grand Hôtel des Étrangers,* and *Fureurs de Mexico.*

Lucien Francoeur (1948): Born in Montreal, he is well known for his recordings of rock music, under his own name or that of the group Aut'Chose, and equally for his work on radio. His songs have appeared under the title, *Rock-désir,* indicative of his concern to marry poetry and rock. Among his books of poetry, one may note *Snack -bar, Drive-in, Les néons las, À propos de l'été du serpent, Une prière rock,* and *Exit pour nomades,* which takes its title from a film by Pierre Bastien.

Normand de Bellefeuille (1949): Born in Montreal, he has published a variety of texts in Herbes Rouges and *La nouvelle barre du jour* that may be said to explore the formal implications of textual theory. He has also written critical articles in *Spirale.* His volume of poems, *Catégoriques un, deux, trois* won the *Prix de la Fondation Les Forges,* and has been translated into English by D.G. Jones as *Categorics, One, Two, and Three* (Coach House Press).

Denis Vanier (1949): Born in Longueuil, he published *Je* at the age of sixteen, with a preface by Claude Gauvreau. He became one of the leading voices of the counter-culture in Quebec, his titles evoking a painful tenderness. Among others, one may note, *Pornographic delicatessen, Lesbiennes d'acid, Le clitoris de la fée des étoiles,* and *L'Hôtel brûlé.* The review *Estuaire* awarded him the *Prix des Terrasses Saint-Sulpice.*

Yolande Villemaire (1949): Born in Saint-Augustin-des-deux-Montagnes, she has produced pieces for radio, several novels, and a number of collections of poetry that include *Du coté hiéroglyphe de ce qu'on appelle le réel, Adrénaline, Les coïncidences terrestres, Jeunes femmes rouges toujours plus belles, Quartz et mica,* and *La lune indienne.* She has also put out a cassette entitled *La montée des anges.* Certainly she is one of the most imaginative writers of her generation. Judith Cowan has translated some of her poems in *Quartz and Mica* (Guernica).

Josée Yvon (1950-1994): Born in Montreal, she became the dark angel of the counter-culture, worked with Denis Vanier, and published short stories and poems, including *Filles-commandos bandées, La chienne de l'hôtel Tropicana, Travesties-Kamikaze, L'âme défigurée,* and *Filles-missiles.* She died of AIDS.

Roger des Roches (1950): Born in Three Rivers, long associated with Herbes Rouges, he is interested in humour, the carnivalesque, the pornographic, among other things, and a good part of his work has been collected in *Tous, corps accessoires.* He works in computer science.

Yves Boisvert (1950): Born in L'Avenir, he has published primarily with Ecrits des Forges. His titles include *Pour Miloiseau, Mourir épuise, Poèmes sauvés du monde,* and *Les amateurs de sentiments.* His *Gardez tout* won the *Prix du Journal de Montréal* and led the film-maker, Robert Desfonds, to produce the movie, *Je ne suis pas rockeur, j'écris.*

Jean-Marc Desgent (1951): Born in Montreal, he has published several volumes with Herbes Rouges and Écrits des Forges, notably *Faillite sauvage, Deux amants au revolver, L'état de grâce, On croit trop que rien ne meurt,* and *Ce que je suis devant personne.* He won the *Prix de la Fondation Les Forges.*

François Charron (1952): Born in Longueuil, he is also a painter and essayist. He is most widely known as a prolific and changeable poet, whose writing has been aggressive, derisive, formalist, Marxist, and, most recently, the expression of a sort of mystical everyday reality, particularly in *L'intraduisible amour.* He is one of the major writers associated with Herbes Rouges. A selection of his recent poems, *After 10,000 Years, Desire,* translated by Bruce Whiteman and Francis Farley-Chevrier was published by ECW Press.

Renaud Longchamps (1952): Born in Saint-Ephrem, he has published, mainly with Herbes Rouge, VLB, and Écrits des Forges, a body of poetry focussed on the material universe and its evolution. The earlier work has been collected in *Anticorps.* The first section of a tryptych, *Décimations,* received the *Prix de la Fondation Les Forges.*

Louis Jacob (1954): Born in Three Rivers, associated with Ecrits des Forges, a novelist as well as a poet, he has engaged in several experiments in collective writing, notably with Yves Boisvert and Bernard Pozier, and he works with the musical group 4K in the presentation of his poetry. His main publications are *Avant-serrure, Sur le fond de l'air,* and *Les noirceurs du corps.*

Marie Uguay (1955-1981): Born in Montreal, she discovered she had cancer and died at a relatively young age, but not before developing a mature poetry, expressing a certain vision of what is essential in life. A kind of retrospective of her work was published by Le Noroît as *Autoportraits,* and a late interview with Jean Royer has been documented on film by Jean-Claude Labrecque A selection of her poems is presented in English translation in *Ellipse,* No. 31.

Bernard Pozier (1955): Born in Three Rivers, he is literary director of Écrits des Forges. L'Orange Bleue has published a selection of his poetry under the title, *Scènes publiques.* He is also the author of a volume devoted to hockey, *Les poètes chanteront ce but.*

Elise Turcotte (1956): Born in Sorel, also a novelist, she has published *La mer à boire, Dans le delta de la nuit, Navires de guerre, La voix de Carla,* and *La terre est ici.* The last two titles earned her the *Prix Emile-Nelligan.*

Hélène Dorion (1958): Born in Quebec City, she is literary co-director of Le Noroît. A selection from her three first books was published by Dé Bleu under the title, *La vie, ses fragiles passages.* A more recent volume, *Sans bords, sans bout du monde,* is published by la Différence. Andrea Moorhead has translated *The Edges of Light: Selected Poems: 1983-1990* (Guernica).

Serge Patrice Thibodeau (1959): Born in Rivière-Verte, in Madawaska, New Brunswick, he has settled in Montreal. He has published *La septième chute* (which won the *Prix France-Acadie), Le cycle de Prague* (which won the *Prix Émile-Nelligan), Le passage des glaces, Le quatuor de l'errance,* and *Nous, l'étranger.*

Louise Blouin (1949): Born in Montreal, she is production manager for Écrits des Forges, as well as a teacher at the Collège de Rosemont. She has published a collection of poems entitled *Griffes de soie* and has edited two anthologies, *Des mots pour rêver* and *De Villon à Vigneault.*

159

Notes on the Translators

Judith Cowan is a translator, a writer, and a professor of English and Canadian literature at l'Université de Québec à Trois-Rivières. She is presently working on a book of short stories.

Arlette Francière, besides translating poems and plays of Henry Beissel and Elizabeth Spencer's novel, *A Bad Cold* into French, has translated a variety of Quebec poets into English. She is also a painter. She lives in Alexandria, Ontario.

Hugh Hazelton is a poet and translator currently living in Montreal. Besides translating contemporary Quebec writers, he has edited several anthologies of Latin American writers living in Canada. He recently translated *Jade and Iron: Latin American Tales from Two Cultures*, edited by Patricia Aldana and published by Groundwood/Douglas & McIntyre.

D.G. Jones is a poet who has translated the work of various Quebec poets, the most recent being Emile Martel's *For Orchestra and Solo Poet* published by The Muses' Co. Retired from l'Université de Sherbrooke, he lives in North Hatley, Quebec.

Monique Martin is a Psychologist who teaches at Champlain College in Lennoxville, Quebec. She has recently translated a major selection of the poems of the Quebec poet, Michel Garneau.

Andrea Moorhead is a poet, translator and editor of *Osiris*, a poetry magazine that features translations from a number of languages. She teaches in the Department of Modern and Classic Languages at Deerfield Academy in Massachusetts.

Sonja Skarstedt is a poet and painter who works as a free-lance graphic illustrator in Montreal. Her latest book of poems is *A Demolition Symphony*, published by Empyreal Press.

Daniel Sloate is a poet, translator and Professor of Linguistics at l'Université de Montréal. Among his many translations one may note Rimbaud's *Illuminations* and Stendhal's *The Life of Mozart*, both published by Guernica.

Philip Stratford is a poet, a noted critic, and an award-winning translator. Recently retired from l'Université de Montréal, where he taught Canadian and Comparative Literature, he lives in Senneville, Quebec.

Donald Winkler was for many years with the National Film Board, where he made a number of films on Canadian poets. He is presently a free-lance film-maker and translator living in Montreal.